TIME OUT WITH AUNT BESS

Expressions of love of family or special time with Aunt Bess

By
Johanna McKenna

TABLE OF CONTENTS

DEDICATION

It is with great pleasure and sorrow that I dedicate "Time Out with Aunt Bess" to the memories of my family. Mom, Dad, Jack, Joan, Gene, and Elizabeth. They all lived with trust in the love and mercy of our beloved God. I must also include the memories of my beloved husband, Frank, and my treasured son, Joseph, who both enjoyed life with love, peace, and joy in the Light of the World.

ACKNOWLEDGMENTS

A special thank you to Frank 2nd and Julia for their encouragement and suggestions.

I would also like to thank Amy and the staff of Lincoln Creative Writers for their help, suggestions, and support.

WELCOME

Welcome to my world. I am Bess, which is short for Bessie. I do not know how that name happened, but I like it. I live with my sister, Helen, and her family. In most of my stories, I refer to her as Mom. Her husband, my brother-in-law, is named John, whom I refer to as Dad. Their children are my nieces and nephews, and I am their 'Aunt Bess.' Do you want to know what I look like? I am not very tall, about five feet three inches, have brownish hair that is turning slightly gray, and enjoy BBQ ribs. Do you want to hear stories? Good, because I enjoy telling all kinds of stories about our life together. Annabelle, Michelle, and Michael like listening to me as I recall our shared adventures.

Annabelle, thirteen years old, smiles as she twists her long brown hair. Wearing her new black-rimmed eyeglasses, Annabelle not only looks serious, she is serious about everything, even meeting me, her Aunt Bess. Michelle, eight years old, is a daydreamer. She likes to write stories and silly poems. Michelle likes people to be happy, which is nice, but her habit of brushing her curly hair is distracting not only to her but also to everyone else. Michelle likes to climb the apple tree in our backyard. Michael, five, has more energy than a lit firecracker and is excited to hear more stories told by me, Aunt Bess. Michael has short brown hair, wears red sneakers, and gets into unusual situations standing still, which is quite often.

Let me explain how this all happened. My sister Helen was married to the love of her life, John. He was extremely sick for a long time, and my sister needed help because she had to return to work while her husband recovered. I came to help her and never left. I became a second mother to Annabelle, Michelle, and Michael. This is enough about me. I know it is time for some stories. Oh, did I tell you? When I came to help, my pet came with me. It came as a surprise when I showed up with "Flossie," my pet pony. Flossie is brown with a white stripe down her back to her tail. She is special in many ways. You will find out as I tell you, what life is like in our family.

Good thing my sister had a two-car heated garage, where Flossie feels right at home. Since it is winter, cold, and snowing, let us begin by telling you about the time Annabelle, Michelle, and Michael went ice skating. They were dressed warmly, wearing scarves around their necks. Flossie wanted to go with them. She had special skates made just for ponies. She had to put on four skates, not just two. They Velcroed together instead of laces. Annabelle and Michelle had their skates on quickly, but Michael was still struggling. They looked up and saw Flossie with tears running down her face.

Michael asked, "Flossie, what is wrong?" Flossie, being a pony, had a genuine problem. "If I put skates on my two front feet, how will I put them on my back feet?" Michelle started to laugh. "You silly pony, put the back ones on first, then the two front ones. You can do it if you try. We will help you if you have a problem. That is what family and friends do. They help each other." Flossie smiled and sat down on the ice. She did manage to put her skates on, but when she stood up, OH, MY! Her legs went in four different directions. Plus, her tail was frozen. Flossie thought, "This is not as easy as I thought." Annabelle, Michelle, and Michael skated over to Flossie, where they quickly removed and wrapped their scarves around Flossie's tail. This made her feel warm, but her legs would not go in the same direction at the same time. The children have an idea, as all children do. They took their scarves off her tail, tied them together, wrapped them around Flossie, and pulled her to safety off the ice. Safety, of course, is the hot chocolate stand. After a hot drink, Flossie defrosts and is ready to try again.

Flossie fell twice, but she did not give up. She starts all over again. This is something we all have to do, especially when we try something new. We do not cry; we do not give up. We start all over again until we succeed. After skating, Annabelle, Michelle, and Michael decided it was time to go home. Mom was baking chocolate chip cookies for them and special ginger cookies for Flossie—it was time to stop for the day.

"Aunt Bess, tell us another story about Flossie," they all said together.

I replied, "Another time. We have many things to complete before your mom and dad return from shopping. First, we have to shovel the snow so your mom and dad have a place to park the car. Right now, it is too deep even to drive up the driveway. Second, we have to build a snowman." Everyone liked that idea. "What should we call him?" asked Michelle. Michael said, "Sam, Sam the Snowman."

Snow is still falling gently as the children and I quickly complete our shoveling. We want to start with Sam. The snow is about three feet deep, and it is cold. The children feel like popsicles but are determined to build their snowman. Annabelle starts with a giant snowball that keeps getting bigger and bigger. Suddenly, they have two giant snowballs, which, when we put them together, are five feet tall. Michael stood on Annabelle's shoulders to wrap a scarf around Mr. Snowman's neck and a baseball cap on his head. We stood back to admire our work. Sam looked good with his baseball cap, scarf, eyeglasses, and long carrot nose. I remind them we must put the shovels away and clean up before we go inside our warm house. Michelle turned to me and asked, "Where is Michael?" The temperature dropped and the snow blew fiercely against our skin. Annabelle shouted, "Michael, Michael, where are you?" Flossie ran to us. I knew it was important because my pony did not like freezing weather. She was pulling on me to go with her. Michelle said, "We better go with your pony. She knows the whereabouts of Michael."

Flossie trotted right to our two-car heated garage, her home. Sure enough, we found Michael warm and sound asleep. My first thought was to join him. Michael looked so comfortable, but we heard a car in the driveway. Mom and Dad had arrived back from shopping. "Sam" was admired, especially his baseball cap (which belonged to Dad). With all the commotion, Michael woke up and asked, "Is dinner ready?" Everyone laughed and said, "Come help." We would soon be enjoying our dinner and dessert: chocolate chip cookies! A perfect end to a perfect day!

That is enough storytelling for now. A new day will bring a new story about Annabelle, Michelle, and Michael. I, your Aunt Bess, will share their childhood adventures and the joy of living God's way.

Rest assured, each tale is a small marvel.

ONE A DAY

Today is a sizzling summer day, and I, Aunt Bess, am helping my sister prepare lunch. Annabelle, with her new black-framed eyeglasses on, is reading "A Pillar of Iron" by Taylor Caldwell. She is thirteen years old and serious about everything. Michelle is brushing her hair, and Michael is sitting on the steps of the front porch. He is watching the new people move into the house next door. So far, he has seen the mother, father, a little boy, and a large shaggy dog. Michael, age five, waves to the boy who looks about the same age as him. He waves back and walks towards Michael. They say "hi" to each other. Michael says, "My name's Michael. What is yours?" "My name is Marcus, and my dog's name is Willie." Michelle is eight years old and wants to meet Willie and Marcus. Michael has two sisters, Michelle and Annabelle. Michelle is always fussing with her brown curly hair. She wants it to be straight, but right now, she wants to meet her new neighbor. She really wants to pet his dog.

Annabelle hears the talking, puts her book aside, walks outside, and introduces herself to Marcus and Willie. Mom and Dad also walk over to welcome their new neighbors. They hope they can become friends. So does Annabelle. Their old neighbors were grouchy and did not like children. Michael and Marcus are soon climbing the apple tree in Michael's backyard. Michael and Marcus are not tall, and both have short dark hair. They quickly discover they love to climb and play outside. The tree has the best branches to sit on. Willie barks louder and louder; he wants to climb and join them. After they climb down, Michael and Michelle take Marcus and Willie to meet Flossie. Marcus had never seen a pony before. He lived in a crowded city. Annabelle is brushing Flossie. She usually takes care of her, making sure there is water, food, and a comfortable place to sleep. Marcus wants to touch Flossie, but he is a little frightened. Annabelle tells him, "Flossie is our pet, just like Willie is your pet. She is bigger; that is the only difference." After a little time, Marcus gathers enough courage to pet Flossie. Flossie likes Marcus and gives him a slight wave of her head. "Do you ever ride Flossie?" he asks. "No, we like her company; she helps us do things around the house. Flossie is like family. We used to ride her, but she is not that young anymore. She not only helps and protects us but also makes us laugh."

Flossie and Willie seem as if they have known each other forever. Mom and Dad invited Marcus and his parents to join us later for dinner. They gladly accepted the invitation. Moving is a traumatic experience, especially from a crowded city apartment to a house in the country. Mom decides that a cookout would be relaxing and fun at the same time. Michael and Marcus are playing catch in the backyard when Michael has an idea. Marcus is not too sure if it is a clever idea, but it sounds fun. It is hot, so, just maybe, it might be all right. Michael slowly walks towards the garden hose and turns on the water. Picking up the hose, he quietly turns it on Michelle. Michelle is asleep in the hammock. She wakes with a startle and does not think Michael is funny. In the meantime, Michael gets everyone wet. Dad is not too happy at the moment. He takes the hose from Michael and proceeds to get him wet. The water is colder than Michael thought, but he laughs so hard that Marcus jumps in front of the water spray. He winds up soaking wet and dripping from head to toe. Flossie and Willie think it would be fun to join them. Mom hears all the noise from the kitchen and comes out to see what is going on. Dad thinks he is funny and turns the hose on Mom. That is a mistake. At first, she is angry, but she starts to laugh when she sees everyone, even Flossie and Willie, dripping water from head to toe or tail. She just says, "That is enough water for one day. Let's all change into dry clothes. At least we will not feel hot for a while."

Marcus runs home to change. He is happy. He thinks, "This is more fun than living in the city. I met a pony, climbed a tree, had a shower with a water hose, and going to have a bar-b-que, all on my first day. I am glad we moved." Marcus, his mom, and dad came over for dinner, carrying a tossed salad and homemade lemonade. The grill is hot, and Dad is busy cooking. As the two families join in a blessing before their meal, you sense friendship. "Michael, Michelle, and Annabelle, I have a surprise for you." They turn and look at Mom. Mom says, "Grandpa Frank is coming to live with us. He will have the big bedroom with the sunporch." Michael is so excited he starts jumping up and down. Michelle and Annabelle give each other the high five. This is really a surprise. Grandpa Frank has been living alone since Grandma went to heaven. Mom and Dad wanted him to live with us forever, or at least it seemed like forever. Michelle is so happy; she is crying. Grandpa Frank is her Godfather. She loves him so much. Annabelle is thrilled. Grandpa Frank is the answer to her prayers. She is studying for Confirmation, and nothing makes sense. Even when Sister Hanna explains the sacrament to her, it is just words that have no meaning. She knows Confirmation is important but does not know why. Grandpa Frank would explain everything. Mom is talking to our new neighbors, telling them all about Grandpa and why we call him Grandpa Frank. Our grandpa is Italian and loves dessert, especially Cannoli. He would go out to dinner with us and order dessert first. Once he ate so much dessert, he had to take his dinner home for the next day. We all laughed so much that when Grandma said, "Frank," at the same time, we said, "Grandpa," and so Grandpa Frank just became his name. It reminds us of the fun we had that night having dinner together.

Dinner is ready; Dad outdid himself on the grill. It is the best hamburger and grilled corn he has ever made. Mom asks if anyone would like coffee or tea with their dessert. Annabelle said, "Yes." Dad and Mom look at her in surprise. "Well, I am making my confirmation soon. I am old enough!" says Annabelle. "Why not," says Dad. "Try a small cup to see if you like the flavor." Michelle and Michael also want to try it... Annabelle tells them, "I do not think I like the taste that much. I will have lemonade instead. You are not missing anything." Marcus And Michael join Flossie and Willie in the yard, where they play catch. The two moms and dads are discussing their work and schools and getting to know each other as friends. As the evening draws to a close, they look forward to a new day after a good night's sleep. Marcus wants to stay overnight at Michael's, but both his mom and dad say, "We are going to spend our first night in our new home together." Michael's mom tells him, "There will be other nights, but the first night is special. God willing, we will see you tomorrow. I am making cookies, and it would be fun if you and Michael help me. I need a stirrer for the batter and a taster when baked. You will have new adventures, at least one a day."

With that as a final word, we all say, "Good night, see you tomorrow."

REFLECTIONS

I, Aunt Bess, am relaxing in my oversized recliner as Michelle and Michael are playing and laughing with Flossie. Flossie, who became our family pet, is loved by every person in our family. She is aging, but our brown pony with a white stripe down her back is still beautiful. Michael, five years old, Michelle, eight years old, and Michael's sister, Annabelle, age thirteen, scolds Michael and Michelle, "You really cannot expect a pony to listen, definitely NOT to pray." I smile and say, "I have a story to tell you. You remind me of the time when Michael and Michelle were standing in front of a big old-fashioned mirror. Michelle was wearing her yellow polka-dotted dress and yellow flowers in her curly hair. Michael had summer shorts covered with red paint. He was painting the garage. His hair was as red as his sneakers and the garage." "Look, there are more people in the room and another pony," Michael yells. Annabelle laughs and tells him, "That is your reflection. You are looking at yourself. That is why it is called a mirror. It is the "mirror" of you. There is only one of you. The second pony reflects Flossie." Michael, a little embarrassed, makes a funny face. Michelle does a silly dance. So does her reflection. "This is fun. Everything we do, our reflection, does the same thing." Michael thinks for a moment and asks, "Does that mean when I have a chocolate ice-cream cone, my reflection has one also?" Annabelle smiles, and her reflection smiles. "Yes, everything you do does reflect you and looks exactly the same."

I am listening to this entire conversation and interjecting a few words, "The mirror reflection only shows what you look like; the real reflection is who you are as a person." I smile and continue, "We should reflect on our blessings. Michael, Michelle, and Annabelle, always remember that true happiness shows our reflections on truth, and the truth is God."

Michael's dad walks over and asks, "Do you know who has been painting the garage? There is red paint on the ground and walls, and even your hair is red." Michael looks up and says, "I want to help.

And no one ever lets me help them. They always tell me, 'You are too little; go play'."

"Michael, you are not old enough to paint the garage alone. I am glad you want to help but wait for a grown-up to be with you. You will grow up soon enough. Do not rush it. You can help me, but first, the paint must be out of your hair."

After an hour of painting, Michael is hungry for lunch, but his dad wants to keep painting. All Michael can think of is a grilled hot dog with relish and mustard, but Michael's dad thinks one more hour, and they will be finished. They have a quiet conversation while they complete the painting, which takes about an hour. "Now, Michael, let's have lunch. That hot dog sounds good, with an ice-cream cone for dessert." My sister, Annabelle's mom, and Annabelle start the grill. They prepared a super summertime meal while the painting was being completed. They sit down to admire their work, only to see a big stripe down the middle of one wall. "Oh, no, what happened?" Flossie walks by, wagging a very red tail. Michael's dad looks like an explosion is about to happen, but my sister begins to laugh. Dad, caught in the contagion of her laughter, soon joins her. He says, "I'll touch it up in the morning." With that problem solved, we enjoy hot dogs and the rest of our dinner. Our conversation becomes serious after dinner.

The conversation concerned our new, deranged educational curriculum when Marcus walked over. Marcus is our next-door neighbor and a good friend of Michael's. I said, "Marcus, have a seat, and how about a hot dog?" Marcus, always with a smile on his face, says, "Sounds good; thank you, Aunt Bess." The conversation continues with real drama when Marcus's parents join us for dessert later in the evening. They have been labeled as terrorists for attending a parent meeting that objected to a new socialist curriculum in the schools. "We are so glad our children are not exposed to indoctrination in the government schools. We feel obligated to make other parents aware of the incorrect teachings of today. It is such a shame this is happening in our country. It is never too late to stop this wave of untruths." Michael and Marcus interrupt the conversation with a bang. They think it would be fun to bring their water pistols and use them on each other. Their parents do not laugh. Michael and Marcus are confined to sitting in chairs opposite each other without their water pistols. They are reminded that there is a time and place for everything. Dinner time is not a suitable time for water pistols! Not too much later, all is forgiven, and today ends peacefully as we all say our good nights to each other.

SUMMER VACATION

Flossie is a strong, intelligent brown pony with a white stripe running from her back to her tail. She is intuitive and notices our emotions when we are near her. Her eyes are incredibly gentle, friendly, and expressive. Flossie is highly protective of us and prioritizes our safety. She is a cherished member of our family, and everyone loves her, even our neighbors. Her stylish sunglasses and favorite hat bob and sway as she trots towards the van.

Michelle, eight years old, is constantly fussing with her hair. Her small hands twist and turn all the curls. Michael is already in the van, sitting beside Aunt Bess. Both are waiting for Flossie.

I love my two baby siblings. They can be trouble sometimes, but I adore them. Me? I am Annabelle, and I am thirteen years old. I love to read. It is always great to have a book with you. There are many times during the day when you have nothing to do; books are a terrific way to spend that time. Besides Aunt Bess's stories, books help me learn things; I have done better in school ever since I started reading more. Anyway, let me move on with what is going on.

Mom and Dad rented a vacation house – on Long Beach Island for the summer. With her wispy, gray hair peeking out of her oversized hat, Aunt Bess will oversee Michael, Michelle, and me while Mom and Dad work on their computers. Aunt Bess is always telling me to write about my experiences in a journal, so I am going to tell you about our experiences at LBI, Long Beach Island... I hope Aunt Bess likes my writing. I hope you like it too.

While driving south on the New Jersey Parkway, Aunt Bess tells us about a giant shark the locals found on the island. I am fascinated by her storytelling skills. I wish to be as good a storyteller as her one day. She told us this shark inspired the movie 'Jaws.'

Aunt Bess says the island is surrounded by water on all sides. The ocean is on one side, and the bay is on the other. During large storms, the water floods the streets. They still tell people to be careful when it is high tide in Beach Haven. Beach Haven is our destination. It is about a three-hour drive from our house to our vacation spot. We turn off the parkway onto Route 72, and from there, we can see the signs for Manahawkin. The latter is the town with the bridge to Long Beach Island. Manahawkin is an Indian name because the Lenape Indians used to live here.

"Are we there yet?" asks Michael for the one-hundredth time.

"Almost," Mom and Dad answer in unison.

"We drove over the causeway. The causeway was the bridge that brings us to the island," Aunt Bess elaborates. She tells us about the seven wooden bridges they crossed before constructing the causeway. It was dangerous but exciting because sometimes water almost covered the bridges. Things are much easier for us now, and we do not have to worry about perilous crossings. An enormous hurricane destroyed the wooden bridges, and a new bridge was constructed. It is called the Causeway, but I do not know why.

We are excited as Dad drives onto the island and heads towards Beach Haven. "This town has the best ice cream, a movie theater, the surf-light theatre, mini golf, and giant sand dunes," we are informed by our dad as he continues to drive.

"Look, there's a pirate ship," shouts Michael. I recall the sailing books I read. It explains how pirate thieves would use their ships to rob travelers in other ships and boats. I know there are pirates even today. I read about them also. Michael is always curious and looking for new adventures, real or imagined. It is a hassle dealing with the fallout, but life is interesting with an adventurous and curious little brother. He has a good habit of asking questions occasionally and keeps asking until he understands the answer. "That is not a pirate ship. It looks like one, but it is a three-masted schooner. Now, it is a gift shop. Her name is Lucy Evelyn," Dad adds for everyone's benefit.

A schooner is a sailing vessel. Dad keeps talking, directing our attention to the beach.

"Look at all the sand. We are going to have so much fun!" says Michelle. Michael and Michelle cannot wait to get out of the van. Flossie is just as excited as the two, wagging her tail. Michelle is fascinated by all the water. The trip to Long Beach Island is her first time seeing the ocean. "It is so huge. I have *never seen so much water.*"

I am lost in my fantasies of sharks and whales, having just completed reading Moby Dick. Looking at the ocean waters, wondering at the unknown lurking beneath the waters, I suddenly become aware of its beauty and power. Aunt Bess takes this moment to comment on the majesty of the ocean. (Our minds must run alike). "The ocean is beautiful, but we must respect its power and mystery. Every wave, great or small, reminds me of the graces that God gives us each moment. The waves never stop moving, and neither does God's love for us. It is eternal. We accept or walk away from it, but He is always there for us, providing untold graces. As each wave rolls onto the sands of the beach, His graces are rolling out for us on the sands of time. We can catch the waves, and we can catch His graces." I am always amazed at how vividly Aunt Bess explains the beauty of nature.

Everyone is quiet, watching the waves roll onto the beach. Michael does not want to stand there, looking at the ocean; he is a man of action. "Let's start digging. I want to build a giant sandcastle." Michael's exclamation brings everyone out of their trance, and we place our towels and beach chairs on the sand. Michael and Michelle dig a hole on the beach so deep that Michael can stand up straight in it. He wants a big castle. The depth of the hole is enough to get Dad a little concerned. "If you go in that hole, the ocean water can fill it, making the sand so wet and heavy that we cannot pull you out. Have you ever heard of quicksand? Fill that in. Shovel the sand back.

Michelle, you know better. You do not have to dig more than a little deep to build a sandcastle."

Flossie is watching them as she slowly walks to the water. The waters roll back and forth onto the beach, tugging gently at her legs while her eyes never leave Michael and Michelle. I am not interested in sandcastles; I watch the ocean waves, wondering at the majesty of the water. Michael is not as interested as I am in this matter. He likes staying busy, prefers activities over meditation, and is too young for such deep thinking. "I'm hungry," he announces.

Mom leaves us on the beach with Dad and Aunt Bess. Someone must prepare lunch. It is usually Mom. Mom makes a big salad with everything in it. Dessert is going to be ice cream – The Beach Haven Special!

Miniature golf is next. Flossie comes to watch us play, but she is not having fun. She lives with only the six of us. Whenever we have company, she observes for a little while before getting comfortable. She is shy. Michelle tells her not to worry, informing her that we will play volleyball on the beach next.

Later, we head back to the beach, put the net up, and prepare for the volleyball game. Mom and Dad make sure the teams are chosen fairly. Flossie is excited to be playing. Soon, everyone on the beach wants to play. Flossie becomes our star player. Her spirit makes her the true winner. She bows whenever her team scores. Everyone cheers for Flossie.

As the day ends, we walk to the other side of the island. We watch a beautiful sunset over the waters of the bay. Dad tells us that tomorrow will be hot because the sun is red today. An open sky means more heat can reach the earth's surface, making the day hotter. There are no clouds to absorb the sunlight. We are too tired to think of tomorrow.

***

Mom and Dad wake us early to see the sunrise over the ocean. It is awesome… You can witness the beauty of God's creation. Early in the morning, all is quiet and calm. The breeze caressing me is cool and crisp. It makes me feel alive and happy.

After breakfast, we are off to the beach. Michael, his pail, and shovel are ready. He is sad when he cannot find the sandcastle he has built yesterday. It disappeared. The beach is covered with small shells. "What happened?" he asks. I explained to him what happened overnight. "When the waves roll in, they knock down whatever is in their way, leave behind what is in the water, roll back, and take the sand back with them. Last night, the waves came, knocked down your castle, left shells, and when they rolled back, they took your sandcastle with them." I watch them run off; then I return to reading 'War of the Worlds.'

I wonder about the heroic actions of the hero in the book. It is remarkable how he was so brave and saved his family in times of extreme danger. He did not give up and stayed strong. I learned how we should not ignore the chance of extraterrestrial existence. Moreover, teamwork is the key in times of conflict rather than fighting over power and resources.

Aunt Bess looks concerned as she watches the lifeguards point to the ocean.

Michelle, wiping her head, "It's hot." She wants to cool off in the water. Flossie wants to do the same. I say, "That is a good idea." Aunt Bess agrees but tells them to stay near the lifeguards. They accompany each other and go frolicking in the water. As the waves roll onto shore, they have fun jumping in them. Flossie is brave as she ventures into the water that comes up to her back. Her tail becomes so heavy with sand and saltwater that it looks like a wet mop. She cannot even lift it.

It is too hot to stay on the beach during the afternoon. Even the sandpipers, tiny birds, scamper all over the beach. They are looking for a place to hide from the sun. We must produce a plan, too.

Something that can save us from the sun's scorching heat, but we can also make the best use of our vacation time. "This is a good time to visit Barnegat Lighthouse," suggests Aunt Bess. Mom and Dad agree. We drive in our van to the lighthouse. It is at the other end of the island.

Fishermen are standing on the rocks near the lighthouse. Fishing poles in hand, they wait and hope for a good catch. It seems like a tough day for them based on the looks registered on their faces. Mom, smiling, tells us about deep-sea fishing. "You join a group on a fishing boat headed for deep waters. The captain navigates. You cast your line and hope for the best. Your father has gone fishing many times. He came home one time with a large fish. The only problem was that he did not have it gutted and ready to cook. I plainly stated that I would cook it but bring it back all cleaned and ready to cook. Much chagrined, he had the fish cleaned and ready to cook." Mom still finds that story amusing. Dad continues to fish, but now he ensures the fish are cleaned thoroughly before bringing them home. When the fishing boats arrive back, people will gut and clean them for you right at the dock. I wonder if Michael has gotten the urge to be always active in his blood from our father.

Looking at the height of the lighthouse, Michelle is having second thoughts about climbing to the top. The lighthouse is 163 feet high. It takes 517 steps to climb that high. That is a lot of stairs to climb. But, as they say, a journey of a thousand miles starts with a single step. And this is just 517 steps, so there are only 516 more to go when you take the first step. The young ones do not understand that they must pace themselves. It looks like they might run up. Mom and Dad both look at Michael and say, "We know you like to climb. Shall we give it a go?" Michael leaps at the opportunity and exclaims, "Let's go to the top."

Michael stops after the two hundred and thirteenth step, but he keeps going all the way to the top. His hunger to explore keeps him going. He continues producing questions regarding the purpose of the lighthouse and who utilizes it. His pursuit of knowledge helps divert our attention from long distances. Though, at times, we must jog our brains and legs to answer his questions. Mom and Dad make sure no one scorned him since it would kill his confidence and curiosity to ask questions. We see all the parks and many boats on the water. We have a perfect bird's eye view of Barnegat. It looks like the fishermen are searching for something. The stairs are much easier going down for Michael and Michelle. It is difficult for Flossie to align her four legs to climb down the stairs. Eventually, the Coast Guard put her in a rubber raft and slid her to the bottom of the stairs.

Mom, Dad, and Aunt Bess come down slowly without any problem. We need a rest after that climb. It is cooler on the beach, so we want to go for a final swim of the day. A sign on the beach says, "No Swimming." We are told the lifeguards have an important meeting, but they will be back. Lifeguards are essential for people's safety in the water. Be it any water body, there is always a chance of an accident that can be fatal. Lifeguards are highly skilled swimmers who can save anyone's life in water. We need a rest, so we are glad to wait.

I return to reading. Michael and Michelle are building a giant fort. Aunt Bess is napping, and Mom and Dad are walking near the water. This is their first time on the beach since we arrived. Flossie, lying on the sand, is dreaming of ginger cookies. The lifeguards come back and take the signs down. The ocean looks inviting, and swimming is allowed. I am looking forward to water skiing. It will be my first time. After trying on the skis and adjusting the straps, I stand on the skis, holding the handle a few minutes later. I am learning how to balance myself. Skimming the water looks like fun. I am sure it will feel fantastic on our feet while the sun is in our faces. I will soon find out!

Flossie is watching as I put on a life jacket. Our intelligent pet pony tries to protect us as much as possible. Flossie's eyes do not leave me as I bend my knees, taking off. The boat is pulling me along the coastline. The wind is in my hair, and it is exhilarating to be on the waters. And then I hear some shouting from the beach. There is a flurry of activity, and everyone on the beach is excited as the lifeguards blow their whistles. I hear them yell, "OUT OF THE WATER NOW. SHARK SIGHTINGS!"

Sharks! Oh, no!

At the mention of sharks, skiing is not fun anymore. The ocean's mysteries are fun to think about but not experience. I have seen too many movies and read books about shark attacks to be comfortable mentioning sharks in the water. The secrets of the water are fantastic to think about, and discovering things about the mystery of the ocean is excellent to learn, but when I think about animals that can hurt you, I get scared. I think about giant octopi, jellyfish that can sting, and other fish with big teeth. I do not want to get in the water when I know about these creatures, especially when sharks are involved.

Flossie stands as tall as a pony can, rushing to the water's edge. Flossie jumps in and swims toward me. The lifeguards are trying to send signals to the boat's pilot. I yell at him, but I do not think he can hear me over the engine. The fishing boats are headed toward me. All the people on the beach are cheering and yelling for Flossie to pull me to shore. The fishing boats reach me at the same time as Flossie. Mom and Dad wonder about all the commotion as they walk back. The men in the boats lift me aboard. They tie a rope around Flossie and hoist her on deck, and she flops on board like a massive fish. The "fishermen" are the coast guard. They patrol the waters to keep everyone safe. When the patrol boats dock, they are greeted with rounds of applause. The lifeguards regret opening the beach: they learned that "decisions bring consequences."

Mom and Dad participate in a candlelight prayer service on the beach that night. Holding hands, we pray, "Thank you, Lord, for protecting us from the dangers of the waters." We hear music as we all say our private words of gratitude to our Lord. Aunt Bess reminds us that even though the Lord created the fish to live in the water, some can challenge us. He is also why we can get through challenging times, share, and use his blessings to counter our fears.

After our prayers are completed, there is time for relaxation. We share food with each other, like a giant picnic involving those who want to join in the fun. The lifeguards brought their guitars so we could have some music afterward. We join them for songs of praise and thanksgiving. Flossie receives the Medal of Honor for fearlessness and bravery.

Water skiing is not on my list of things to do anymore, at least not soon. Hopefully, in the future, I can get over my fear and participate in activities involving the water. I will go diving near the coral reef I read about when there are no sharks. For now, I will enjoy the beach more than the water. Michael and Michelle build sandcastles, and I walk along the beach. Eventually, I overcame the fear and recovered enough to relax and enjoy the summer vacation. Life becomes calmer as we settle into life at Beach Haven. Mom and Dad finish their computer work and join us for fun and sun on the beach. Never at a loss for words, Aunt Bess has a story for every day, which becomes part of the wonders of summer life at the Jersey shore.

Time rapidly passes when you are having fun, and we are soon left only with summer vacation memories. A few weeks of sun and ocean with summer activities and good food has left us refreshed and rejuvenated for the rest of the year.

I cannot wait for our next adventure.

PIZZA DAY

The doorbell rings, and Michael runs to the door. It is Grandma with two giant suitcases. Grandma is staying for the weekend. It is Friday, and at our house, it is pizza day. Grandma has surprises in one suitcase, something special for everyone, but we must wait for the right moment. That is what Grandma always says, "There is a right moment for everything." We must wait for the moment, but that is okay. That one suitcase is heavy. I wonder what is in it. "Guess what, Grandma, we are having pizza tonight, your favorite." Michael, five, wishes every day were pizza day, not just Friday. Annabelle, thirteen, wearing dark-rimmed eyeglasses, is explaining to Michael that it would not be special if we had pizza every day. Michael did not want to know about all that. He knows Grandma is here, and that is special enough for him.

Michael knows the first thing they would do is give each other your great big grandma hugs. They always make you feel special and loved. The second thing is Grandma's tea. It must be herbal without milk, and it must be hot. After all the other talking is finished, the big moment finally arrives. The third thing and the real reason for Grandma's visit is that Grandma and Michael will make chocolate-chip cookies. Michael likes grandma's cookies. She makes them just the right size. Michael has grandma's recipe almost memorized. He knows where Mom keeps the mixing bowls. Michael runs to get the bowls and the eggs while Grandma finds the flour and sugar. "Do not drop the eggs," says Grandma. "I will be careful, Grandma." He places the bowls on the counter with the eggs right next to them. As he turned to help Grandma, one egg rolled onto the floor. "Oh no, I was so careful." "Not to worry," said Grandma. "It could have been worse. We have more, thank goodness. Just try to be more careful next time. Michael. We better check the recipe before we start," says Grandma. "First, we set the oven at 350 degrees. We line our cookie sheets with parchment paper. Then, we begin mixing. We will do the butter and eggs first. Make sure the butter is soft enough to mix with the eggs,

Michael. Do you remember how much we need? You better read the recipe aloud. That will help us remember."

one cup butter (softened)

one cup of white sugar

one cup of brown sugar

two tsp vanilla extract

two eggs

three cups white flour

one tsp baking soda

one tsp baking powder

three cups of chocolate chips

Sift the dry ingredients together!

Mix the butter, eggs, and vanilla.

Add flour mixture a little at a time.

Stir in chocolate chips with a wooden spoon. Do not overmix!

"Okay, Michael. We are ready to make our cookies. Should we make little or giant cookies?" asks Grandma. "Giant," says Michael instantly. "Let's start," says Grandma. Michael and Grandma measure everything carefully. They follow the directions step by step and wind up with cookie dough. Using a large serving spoon, one by one, a giant spoonful of cookie dough is scooped onto the parchment paper. One cookie sheet at a time is placed in the oven for ten minutes. They make giant cookies; it takes fourteen minutes to cook. They wait ten minutes for them to cool. They carefully place them on a plate reserved for grandma's cookies. Michael is the taster. With a mouthful of cookies, he has a big smile as he, with a little help from Grandma, is busy preparing the next tray for the oven. When all the cookies are completed, and there are a lot of them in varied sizes, Michael has his third with a glass of milk. Grandma has one with another hot cup of tea. Mom, Dad, Michelle, and Annabelle join them for a cookie party. "Annabelle and Michelle, where have you been? You disappeared while we were cooking. That is not like you. The house was so quiet this afternoon. We missed you," says Grandma lovingly.

"We are sorry, Grandma, but we were helping Flossie. Flossie, our pony and family pet, was digging to help start our garden. We have been talking about a rock garden with different flowers growing between the rocks," says Annabelle.

"That sounds like a promising idea. Very interesting," says Grandma. "This is a good moment. While everyone is here, I would like to give each of you something I pray you will cherish and keep in our family forever." Grandma pauses and addresses Annabelle, "Annabelle, would you and your dad please bring my other suitcase here? I cannot carry it. It is too heavy." As the suitcase comes, Grandma opens it slowly and carefully withdraws one package wrapped tightly. She says, "Annabelle, this is a treasure from your great-grandpa. It has been in our family for years and has the record of every child since his generation. The family bible. This is the only record of our family. You are now entrusted with written records of our heritage. You can add the names of this generation. Include your cousins. Michelle, you are receiving a pure gold cross that was your great-grandmother's. She received it from her great-grandpa as a special gift when your grandpa was born. I know you are too young to wear it, but I want you to have it. Your mom will keep it for you until you are older. Michael, this is a telescope to help you see the stars and moon at night. Great-grandpa loved to look through it and wonder about the beauty of life. Also, there is a baseball that was great grandpa's when he played for the Brooklyn Dodgers. It is old, so do not play with it; treasure the memories that go with it. Think about Great Grandpa in his baseball uniform. This is what made my suitcase heavy. I did not know you were building a rock garden, but this fits your project perfectly. You now have Grandma's Statue of the Blessed Mother. This originally was in your great-grandmother's front yard in Roselle, N. J. There is quite a story behind this statue. At that time, members of the Klu Klux Klan lived in this small town. And they did not like Catholics. When your great Grandma placed the statue in her front yard, Grandpa built a gate around it so it could not be broken. They would burn crosses right next to the statue. Your great-grandmother would take her broom and, with sheer determination, bang her broom against the flames until she succeeded, and the fire became burnt ashes. Her anger gave her the needed strength. It happened more than once, but after the police and fire department became involved, the fires stopped. You could call it Mary's Garden if you like the idea. Think about it."

We all say in one breath, "It's a perfect name."

"I have more gifts with me. Where is Aunt Bess? She has been missing the entire day," asks Grandma.

"She went shopping. They are having a 60% off sale, and you know Aunt Bess and sales," says Mom. Grandma laughs and says, "I do not blame her. Everything is so expensive these days. In the meantime, I have something for Flossie. We can hang this sign right on her front door. Everyone can see and read it. A wooden heart with the words inscribed on it: 'PEACE…LOVE…. JOY.' Flossie brings this to our family. When I went on the pilgrimage to Fatima last year, I purchased blessed rosaries. Aunt Bess, Uncle Joe, Aunt Beth, your other uncles, aunts, and cousins will each receive a rosary from Fatima. We could all say the rosary together in Mary's Garden when it is completed." Everyone seemed mesmerized by Grandma's talk.

"That is a good thought. Let us do it." Aunt Bess walks into the house as Grandma is closing her suitcase. "Just in time," says Grandma. "You are going to now have a blessed rosary from Fatima. When you visit the rest of the family, please bring these rosaries to them for me." Grandma also bought a new collar for Turbie, Uncle Joe's farm dog. He guards the sheep and the farm. It has his name on it with an angel beside it. He is a guardian for all of us.

Now, Grandma's suitcase is empty, and the moment has arrived for pizza. Mom ordered three different pies, and Dad picked them up. After dinner, Michael sits in the yard with his new telescope, watching for the stars and moon to appear in the darkness of night. After cleaning up the kitchen, Mom and Dad join Michael outside. Dad starts a fire in the fire pit, and one by one, the family trickles outside. Michael is so excited. He is looking at the moon and can see a man's face. Dad wants to explain about the craters and different stars, but that will wait for another time. Michael is excited enough over the moon, and he is only five. Besides, there is a growing cry for smores from the rest of the family. Mom, I, Aunt Bess, and Annabelle make smores for Grandma, Dad, and Aunt Beth. Relaxing until it is past bedtime, we finally say good night, looking forward to another day with Grandma. Michael is so tired that Mom carries him to his bed. Michael whispers in Mom's ear, "Do you think we can have pizza tomorrow?" He falls asleep before he hears the answer.

A SPECIAL GIFT

Annabelle, Michael, and Michelle's Mom and Dad are preparing breakfast. Sunday is always special—blueberry waffles or, sometimes, strawberries. Mom is cooking the waffles while Dad is defrosting the bacon.

I am Aunt Bess, and I am telling you about the wonders of living with my sister's family. Annabelle, Michelle, and Michael continue their adventures; I will tell you about them. There is a story within every adventure.

Annabelle, thirteen, and her little brother, Michael, five years old, catch the aroma of breakfast in progress. Even Flossie, our pet pony, meanders near the house. She cannot have any, but she does like the aroma. After breakfast, we get ready for church. Michael asks his mom if Marcus, his new friend, can accompany them. She tells Michael he could ask but does not know if they go to the same church. To everyone's surprise, Marcus, his mom, and Dad are ready for church. This will be their first time at St. Joseph's, just like Grandpa Frank. They ask Mom what we should call Marcus' Mom and Dad. Marcus' mother said, "How about Dr. Watkins and Mrs. Watkins?" Our mom said, "OK, Marcus, you can call us Mr. and Mrs.Spruce."

After church service, Dad introduces our new friends to Father Murphy, and he welcomes them to St. Joseph's parish. We are on our way home when Michelle starts crying. "What is wrong?" we all ask. "I do not know. I just feel sad," replies Michelle. "I know why," said Michael. "You must play with Willie, Marcus' large shaggy dog, and Flossie. They will make you forget about feeling sad. Besides, Mom is making cookies today. You can help Marcus, who will help me while I help Mom."

I join in, "Michael is right. Everyone can use help." Grandpa Frank also put in his thoughts, "No time to be sad. There is too much to be done. Today is the perfect day to have a cookie party. We will celebrate life at our house." Michael knows where his mom keeps the flour and sugar. Michael is so anxious to start that he takes the flour and sugar off the cabinet shelves. "Be careful," said Michelle. "Let me help you." With that, the flour lands on the floor, but Marcus catches it in time. As for the sugar, it lands with a plop. The bag splits open, and it makes quite a mess. Michelle cleans it up as best she can. They wait for Mom to appear, which she does out of nowhere.

"Michael, you must learn patience. It is a good thing we have extra sugar. I know you want to help, but all good things take time. Now, let's find the recipe."

After a while, "Here it is," said Mom.

one cup butter

one cup sugar

one cup of brown sugar

two tsp vanilla

two eggs

three cups flour

1 tsp baking soda

½ tsp baking powder

two cups of chocolate chips

Sift dry ingredients! Mix butter, eggs, and vanilla. Stir in dry ingredients, stir in chocolate chips (with a wooden spoon), and cook at 350 degrees for about ten minutes (unless you make giant ones). Let them cool for about five minutes, and transfer to a special cookie plate. Have a cookie party!

"Marcus, how are you at measuring? Have you ever done it before?" I ask. "There is a first time for everything. Let us learn, Michelle. Show Marcus."

"Michelle, you read the recipe and tell them how much of each ingredient is needed."

"Annabelle, you are the supervisor. Make sure the measurements are correct."

"I will prepare the cookie sheets and turn on the oven."

Grandpa Frank is getting ready for the cookie party. Michael and Marcus are stirring the batter when they hear a loud clap of thunder and a fierce bolt of lightning across the sky. Marcus jumps and becomes frightened. Grandpa Frank says, "Do not be scared. It only means the angels are bowling, and one got a strike."

"Are you sure?" asks Marcus. "Absolutely, Michael's grandma told me that, and she knew all about angels."

"How are those cookies coming along?" asks Dad. "They sure smell good." Mom pulls the last tray out of the oven at that moment. "These are the giant ones. One is for Michael, and one is for Marcus. They take fifteen minutes longer to cook."

"They smell so good. Michael, please hand me the cookie plate. Michael, Marcus, where are you? You both help clean up. That is an important part of cooking."

There is a strange noise from Flossie's house, our two-car heated garage. It is raining, coming down in buckets. Michael and Marcus run into the house. They are as wet as can be. "We saw an angel. Grandpa Frank was right. They were bowling. Our angel fell out of the sky." Mom looks at them. "Where did you see the angel?" "Right by Flossie's house. We heard the noise and went to see what happened. There he was, only he did not have any wings." "Michael, that too is quite a story. Show me where you saw your angel after it stops raining." I think about Michael and his angel, "He did see an angel. That would be impressive. I will pray about it." The rain stops, and Mom goes to check on the angel story. Flossie is there looking happy and content with life. Mom tells Michael he has quite an imagination since no one else, including Marcus, saw an angel.

Michael knew what he saw and will treasure that moment forever. Michelle, Michael, Mom, Dad, and Grandpa Frank are enjoying their cookie party when there is another loud noise. This time, both Dad and Mom jump up. The giant oak tree in front of our house had come crashing down. It missed our home by just about two inches. Michael and Marcus run outside to climb in the branches. They cannot even climb over the trunk of the fallen tree. It is that big. Dad tells Michael and Marcus to be careful as they play hide and seek in the tree's large branches. Grandpa Frank is in charge for now.

Mom leaves for work, and Dad drives Annabelle to her class. Father Murphy is teaching a special class for confirmation. Annabelle is late and rushes to her seat as Father Murphy is explaining the need to know about the seven gifts of the Holy Spirit. He explains to the class that they are becoming adult members of their religion. It is a time to be serious and learn as much as they can. They also must do a service project. That means helping others as an act of charity or love. Having your parents, older brother, or sister help you is good. Father Murphy tells them to get a copybook to write down what they were doing, why it was done, and who they helped. Also, keep track of the hours spent helping people. The next thing is a confirmation name. They have to know about the saint, what their name signifies, and why they picked that saint. Father Murphy writes the words FEAR OF THE LORD on the board. He asks us why this would be a gift. We all have different answers, but the best is another question: Why should we be afraid? Our pastor smiles and says, "We should fear anything that could bring us to sin because sin will keep us from seeing God. Be afraid of sin."

Father Murphy writes one more word on the board. Piety. He explains, "This special gift helps us love God as the Father and obey Him because we love Him. The rest of the class talks about service projects. Our neighbor is elderly. Annabelle thinks she can clean her house and take care of her lawn. She can use help and a friend. Someone else suggests the food bank. Father Murphy tells us to always ask our parents to help us. "That is part of your service project. Ask for help," he says.

As we leave, Father Murphy reminds the class to choose a name for confirmation. Dad picks Annabelle up and is in a hurry to get back home. He tells her Grandpa Frank was playing with Michael and Marcus when he got stuck on a branch. It seemed like quite a predicament. When they arrive home, Grandpa Frank, Michael, and Marcus sing "God Bless America" at the top of their voices. Instead of being upset over something as silly as being stuck in a fallen tree, Grandpa Frank says, "We should be grateful for the tree. Look at all the happiness this tree has given us. We had shade outside on a sizzling summer day, and it made our house cooler at the same time. And I know you will all miss raking up all those leaves in the Fall."

"After your dad and Uncle Joe cut all the big logs into smaller logs, there will be enough wood for both families. For all winter and then some," says Grandpa Frank to Annabelle. Grandpa Frank can always make something good come out of everything and anything (almost). He calls it being wise enough to see the splendor of God's creations. He says some people think they are greater than God. They are either crazy or sitting among the lost souls. Our tree is indeed a gift from God, I think. I will miss its beauty and climbing in it as Grandpa Frank says, "Enough talk. Get me out of here. These branches are too big. I need help." Michael and Marcus are not any help at all. They think it is funny to be stuck in a tree.

Uncle Joe and Aunt Beth (which is short for Elizabeth) have a hundred-acre farm. It is enormous. We often stay there and have great fun.

I think, "This a real emergency service project." Dad cut the smaller branches off the tree while I tried to get Grandpa Frank to free his leg. He is stuck in between two branches. Michael says, "I will ask my angel to help." Michelle tells him, "I do not know if your angel can. He is your imaginary angel, but we can ask Grandpa Frank's angel to help him." Michael replies, "I will ask both." I know Michael's prayers worked quicker than Dad's saw. He could only cut one branch at a time when Grandpa Frank suddenly stood up on both legs with my help. With a loud voice, he declares, "Time for our cookie party." Dad, Mom, Annabelle, Michelle, Michael, Marcus, and I agree with Grandpa Frank. Today is special. We received the gift of no one being hurt by a fallen tree, especially Grandpa Frank. The cookies taste extra good. Annabelle thinks, "My Mom is going to be my sponsor, and Eulalia is an old family name that fascinates me. I must do research before next week. For now, I am enjoying my family and our cookies."

"Batter Up!" I say. I am sitting in my favorite rocking chair, reading one of my favorite books, "Theophilos" by Michael O'Brien. I am not very tall; I have deep blue eyes, and I am told I have an incredibly happy and warm smile. That never made sense to me. Why would I smile if I were not happy? Putting my book down and looking up, I see three faces looking right at me. "Would you like to hear another story?" I ask. Michael nods, "Yes," while Michelle and Annabelle nod in agreement.

"Where's Flossie?" asks Michelle. Michelle, eight years old, is brushing her curly hair. Michael is now five, and his sister, Anabelle, is the oldest at age thirteen. Michael chimes in, "Where's Flossie?" Michael has more energy than a lit firecracker. He is climbing the apple tree when he thinks of Flossie. Annabelle, wearing dark-rimmed glasses, is holding her new book, "The Diary of Anne Frank."

"This story is real," she thinks. "What if I had lived in Germany at that time? I could have been just like Anne. I am going to ask Aunt Bess about this. She has traveled to Germany many times. She can tell me more about the book as it relates to history." That thought stayed with her. With a big smile, I say, "Flossie, this is not funny. Where are you?" Flossie is waking up from her nap in her house (our two-car heated garage). She thinks to herself, "I am right here. Where else would I be?" Flossie, our unique family pet, a pony with a white stripe right down to her tail, thinks, "So much noise."

"Now that I am awake, we must play. It is a beautiful day. Annabelle, Michelle, Michael, what game should we play?" Annabelle thinks, "I really want to read my new book, but I want to ask Aunt Bess about it first. I can read it later after she tells me about life during the war." Annabelle says, "You are right. It is a beautiful day. We can play pretend baseball." The bases are set, and boundaries are met. Michael is ready and holds the bat steady. Annabelle throws the ball. "Strike one." Michael swings and misses. Another throw. Michael swings and makes a hit. The ball only goes a little bit. "Strike two." Michael swings again and misses. "Strike three." He is only five.

Michelle is next. She stands tall … bat in hand, she is ready. We stand and watch. "Strike one." "Strike two." "Strike three."

"Oh, no! Let us put an end to this nonsense!" Now it is Flossie's turn to bat. She just sits. Annabelle says, "Flossie, you must try." Flossie let out a big sigh. "BATTER UP!" is the cry. All we hear is another big sigh. Flossie holds the bat. "Strike one." … "Strike two." When that last ball flies right unexpectedly, Flossie runs to the first and second, "RUN, FLOSSIE, RUN!" Third, she passes into home plate and slides. What cheers from the crowd! (Just us). "Home run! Home run!"

Flossie is so proud. We must celebrate Flossie's big win. Flossie gives a great pony grin. She turns to Annabelle and says, "I am glad you made me try. Thank you for making me part of your family."

I, Aunt Bess, watch the whole game from my rocking chair. "Congratulations on your win. You are quite extraordinary. Ice cream for all with whipped cream and chocolate syrup."

After we all settle down with our ice cream, Annabelle brings up the question of the war in Germany to Aunt Bess.

"Why do you want to know about World War Two?" I ask. "It was a horrible time started by a madman—Hitler," I tell Annabelle. "You are about to read the thoughts of a young girl who was thirteen years old. Anne Frank and her family hid from the Nazis for years. It is true; Anne's diary of the atrocities of the war are all true. We find it hard to believe that this happened, but it did. More people should read about the wars to prevent them from happening again. History repeats itself, and it is easy to lose democracy. When you read "The Diary of Anne Frank," you go back in time and read about World War II. You will learn what can happen in any country when the people do not pay attention to what their leaders are doing to their country. Annabelle, this is a serious subject for a summer afternoon. I am glad to hear about your interest, but for now, enjoy reading the thoughts of a young girl. It will help if you write your ideas down when you finish. Your lives are different. I hope and pray they will always be as happy as today is for all of us."

Michael is ready for another game. He is the only one who wants to play. "I suggest that one game a day is enough. Now, we must rest our bodies and spend more time with your Aunt Bess. Be strong." I smiled. "Another story? Absolutely. Get comfortable and listen while we go to the zoo." "Aunt Bess is never tired of her amazing storytelling," thinks Annabelle.

Annabelle, Michelle, and Michael are anxiously waiting for Grandpa Frank. He is taking them to the National Washington Zoo. Mom and Dad are also going. Michael, five years old with a mischievous smile, wants to see a giraffe, and Michelle wants to see the zebras. Anabelle, since she is only thirteen, really wants Grandpa Frank to help her. She is making her confirmation next weekend and wants to make sure she understands the sacrament. Grandpa Frank is so brilliant. She always asks him questions. He will look up the answers with her if he is not sure of the answer. Grandpa Frank always tells her, "It doesn't hurt to double-check."

Confirmation is next week, but seeing the lions and tigers will be fun. Grandpa Frank wants to see the elephants. He tells Annabelle, "Do not worry. I will answer all your questions after we visit the zoo."

34

WISDOM ANSWERS

It will be an exciting day for all of us. We are going to see more than they expect. I think they have at least three hundred and fifty kinds of animals. When we arrive, we walk through the gate and see a giant lion statue. Michael is so excited that he starts to run down the first path. Mom runs after him, "Michael, stay with us. This is a large zoo, and you will get lost. We will see the animals and learn about them, too."

Michelle, who is eight years old, grabs Grandpa Frank's hand as they walk towards the animals. Michael lets out a yell, "Look! Over there. It is an elephant." Sure enough, there are not one but eight elephants enjoying the outside air while munching on the grass (at least that is what it looks like). As we continue our walk into this fantasy wonderland that provides for these animals, we are amazed at how the animals have a house or cave to live in when it rains or snows, it gets too hot or cold. They can live inside or outside.

Grandpa Frank and Michelle are still watching the zebras. The pandas enthrall Annabelle. Dad wants to see the snakes, and Mom is frantic. She cannot find Michael. She tells Dad, "Forget the snakes for now. We must find Michael." Michael is watching the giraffes and becomes so engrossed in their height that he forgets where he is for a minute. He turns around, and he is alone. "Where did everyone go?" he wonders. "This is scary; I do not want to be alone." Annabelle is right behind him, but he is not aware of it. "Michael, I am right here. Michael, I am right here." Michael rushes to his big sister and gives her a big hug. "I wasn't scared," says Michael. "I just do not want to be alone." "Let's go find Mom." Grandpa and Michelle walk over and join us in finding Mom. Mom and Dad are frantic. They cannot find anybody. After a fruitless search, they look and say to each other, "Maybe we are the ones who are lost." They suddenly hear a noise, turn, and see Grandpa Frank, Michelle, Annabelle, and Michael walking towards us. Grandpa Frank and Michael ask, "What's for lunch?" Mom and Dad say, "We must stay together for the rest of the day. It is not fun to look for anyone who is lost, especially in this giant zoo."

Grandpa Frank tells us, "We are not lost. You better stay with us. We can explore more after lunch." After lunch, we decide to find the gorillas. Mom, Dad, Annabelle, Michelle, Michael, Grandpa Frank, and me, Aunt Bess all start walking together to find the part of the zoo with the gorillas. We walk and walk until Michelle says, "Look over there." We turn and see a big enclosure with a giant gorilla inside. He looks sad. Our heads turn to see a man throwing wads of paper at him. The man keeps throwing things at him over the fence. He even throws an empty can of soda. Dad is about to walk over to him when one of the workers approaches him and tells him, "Do not do anything yet. Jack, my gorilla friend, can manage this." We stand and watch as Jack gathers the papers and empty cans with a handful of dirt and grass. His back faces the man, so he cannot see what he is doing. It looks like he is cleaning his space. After Jack gathers everything into a big pile, he turns, faces the man, and throws it. Everything lands right in his face. They stand there laughing and applauding. Chagrinned, the man disappears. The worker says, "What did I tell you? My friend, Jack, can take care of himself." At that point, we are ready to leave for home, with a promise of spending another day at the zoo.

Once we arrive home, everyone is tired except Annabelle. She is making her confirmation this weekend and is excited. She wants to talk to Grandpa Frank about her confirmation. He is tired, but Annabelle reminds him of his promise. She wants to know how the gifts of the Holy Spirit have anything to do with life. Grandpa Frank looks at Annabelle and tells her, "Think about today and everything that happened. We had fun being together as a family. You kept an eye on your brother without even telling him. We watched that man doing cruel things to an animal and saw what happened."

"Grandpa Frank, what has that got to do with confirmation?" Annabelle inquires. "I am tired, but this is important. Use your head. What are the gifts of the Holy Spirit?" says Grandpa Frank. Annabelle knows what they are but cannot see why it is so important to know them. Grandpa Frank tells her, "If we did not have these gifts, the devil would deceive us in everything we do. Remember, he is knowledgeable and has been alive for a long time. He knows how to trick people into believing his lies. Before I fall asleep, tell me what they are and what they mean to you?" Annabelle thinks and begins narrating the whole list, "Wisdom, understanding, knowledge, counsel and ..." "Now, wait a minute, Annabelle," says Grandpa Frank. "Slow down; what does wisdom mean to you?"

"It means being smart in everything we do."

"You are right, but it is more than that. We desire to do what is right because our whole life is doing what is right for ourselves and for the honor and love of God and His commandments. You can recognize all your gifts through understanding and knowing the difference between good and evil, right and wrong, and lies and truth. It is also knowing when to speak and when not to speak. That is especially important. You have the wisdom to watch over Michael, protect him, and help him. You helped him bolster his courage, yet you did not have to say anything. I hear you talking to Michelle and Michael, telling them what is right and wrong, just like your mother and father told you. You knew it was wrong for that man to throw anything at Jack, the gorilla. How did you know? How was your dad strong enough to want to talk to that man about what he was doing? That is the gift of fortitude. He was going to do what was right. Did we cover all the gifts?"

"No, there are two more. Piety and fear of the Lord," says Annabelle.

"What do you think they mean, and how did we use them today?" asks Grandpa Frank. "I do not understand them. I am not afraid of God; I love Him. He has given me a lot," Annabelle answers. Grandpa Frank smiles and tells Annabelle, "You must always stay the same as you are now. You love your God and do not want to commit any sin to make Him sad or angry. You watched and protected Michael today and helped your family enjoy being together. This is what it is all about. This weekend, you will receive the Sacrament of Confirmation—a special grace from God that will strengthen your faith. This sacrament will grant you the wisdom to live the gifts of the Holy Spirit. Annabelle, you will have more questions as you continue to grow older. We will find the answers together. Look around you. Usually, the answers are right in front of us. We must see to accept them. You must be strong in the truths of your beliefs. Annabelle, I am exhausted, and I am going to bed. I suggest you do the same. Everyone else is asleep. Tomorrow is a new day. Good night and sweet dreams."

"You too, Grandpa Frank," says Annabelle.

SAINT FRANCIS AND FLOSSIE

I, Aunt Bess, am sitting in my favorite rocking chair on the front porch, reading a book and drinking lemonade. Annabelle, wearing her black-rimmed glasses, is helping Michael carry a tray of chocolate chip cookies to the porch. Michelle, eight, soon joins them after brushing her hair as usual. I have a big smile for them as they share the cookies with me, "My favorite. Do you know Sunday is the Feast of Saint Francis?" I ask them. "Who is Saint Francis?" asks Michelle. "He is the patron saint of animals. I am reading about him now. Francis was born in Italy. He was extraordinarily rich and very spoiled. When he was older, he became a soldier to fight in the wars. Francis was hurt badly, and his life began to change. He shared his wealth with the poor and began to live a life of poverty. He tried to preach about God's love, but people, at first, did not listen. So, Francis spoke to the fish, the birds, and all the rest of the animals. One day, he was missing from home. Everyone looked for him. They found him talking to the wolves. He told the wolves, 'The village will feed you if you stop eating all the chickens.' Saint Francis would talk to all the animals. Birds would perch on the branches of trees. Wolves would lay gently on the ground when he spoke to them about God's love."

"I know that tomorrow is Sunday. It is also the Feast Day of Saint Francis. People bring their pets for a blessing. Saint Francis loved all animals. They will have the service and blessing outside. I think Flossie should go," I suggest as I see Flossie running toward us. Our brown pony with white stripes down her back is on her way. Her big brown eyes sparkle while her white tail sways back and forth. We all smile. Another new adventure is about to begin.

I continued, "Saint Francis was able to see God. He performed miracles to help people. I do not understand all of this. Life is a mystery sometimes. We must have the knowledge, but we still must also live on our Faith," I tell them as they listen with attention. Sunday is a special day. This year will be extra special. "Flossie, this is Sunday and Saint Francis Day." Flossie love animals. "You should come with us today." I pet Flossie. While we are getting dressed for church, the plea for Flossie to come with us can be heard, "Flossie, come with us. Our cousins will be there with their pets." Flossie becomes excited. She has never been to a church. She knows it is important. The church is nearby, so we walk, and Flossie follows. Chairs are set up outside. Our cousins are already there. We sit next to them. Flossie stands right next to us.

Frank, their oldest cousin, is allergic to animals. He has his fish in their fish tank right on his lap. Greg has his big dog, and Bernadette is holding a birdcage, with her yellow canary, tightly in her hands. The service starts. We bow our heads in prayer. Flossie bows her head. She understands the reverence and power of prayer. Frank sneezes thirty-two times; the fish are quiet, and Greg's dog barks loudly. Bernadette's canary never stops chirping. The pastor gives a short talk on living God's way. It must be short---too much competition! Finally, the blessing. We stand by Flossie. Frank holds his goldfish bowl. Bernadette holds her birdcage, and Greg holds his dog. We and our pets are sprinkled with holy water with the words, "Thank you, God, for all your creations – The birds, the fish, the dogs, and Flossie. May you all be blessed by your creator, and may you find happiness and joy in your owners. Amen."

Flossie smiles as if saying, "Want to race home?"

"No way," we all say together. "You always win." Michelle, Michael, Frank, Greg, Bernadette, Annabelle, and I, Aunt Bess, all walk to Grandpa's home to celebrate together. Sunday dinner is ready. Spaghetti, meatballs, salad, garlic bread, and a special Saint Francis dessert! "Aunt Bess, what is a Saint Francis dessert?" asks Michelle. I tell them, "I know it is an Italian pastry, a type of cookie. Almond biscotti are good also. Flossie, you can have your dinner and a special ginger snap cookie for your dessert. Let us bow our heads and offer thanks."

"Love, peace, and joy."

I feel happy. I know St. Francis would have enjoyed today. He would have loved an Italian dinner, especially the desserts. Flossie smiles as she shakes her head in agreement. Aunt Bess, that is me. I am sitting in my favorite recliner, reading a book, but I enjoy listening and watching my family. It is such a joy to be a part of them. They do not realize the happiness I feel in my heart. Michael and Michelle are becoming impatient with Annabelle. All she talks about is her new confirmation name. Eulalia is unusual, but she likes the name. Michael wants to play with Marcus, his neighbor and friend. Michelle, eight years old, wants to go to sleep. She is tired after helping Grandpa Frank hunt for lost tennis balls. He is determined to find every tennis ball that the players hit out of the court. The tennis courts are about a block away from where we live. Grandpa Frank likes to watch them play. He does not understand the game, but he thinks it is fun to see how they run after the tennis ball and slam it. He laughs when they miss hitting the ball. I do not think they like Grandpa Frank to watch them. Michelle and Grandpa Frank found twenty-six tennis balls. They did have fun looking for them, but Michelle was tired. She did all the searching while Grandpa Frank told her where he thought they landed. Annabelle is having another lesson from Father Murphy on Confirmation. He wants to know if the students have chosen their confirmation names yet. Annabelle tells him she is still thinking of Eulalia. "Hmm, that is an unusual name. Where did you hear the name?" he asks. "It is an old family name. I heard my uncle and aunt talk about Eulalia last year. The name fascinates me, but I do not have information on St. Eulalia yet. I will, by next week."

Annabelle really wants to be home. Mom was supposed to make cookies with Michael and Marcus today, but that must wait. There is an emergency at work, and she has to leave. Grandpa Frank is going to show us how to make pizza. Annabelle hopes he will wait for her to come home. Michelle is asleep on the couch, but Michael is ready for a new adventure. He is impatient and wants to start making pizza this minute. "Michael, we will make the tomato sauce. That takes more time than anything else. You take out the big pot." At the same time, I open six cans of tomatoes. "Mom and Dad can freeze whatever is left."

Michael hopes he is right. Grandpa Frank opens three cans of tomato sauce and three cans of chopped tomatoes and dumps all the tomatoes into the big pot. "Michael, we need basil and garlic to give the sauce flavor. Peel the garlic, press the juice into the sauce, wash the basil, and put it in the sauce." Michael says, "Grandpa Frank, we should wait for Annabelle and Michelle." Grandpa Frank agrees, "You are right. We can clean the kitchen. There is a mess here. This was your idea, Michael. Help me rinse out all these cans. You can put them in the recycling bin." Just then, Annabelle walks in as the last can is going in the bin. Dad and Mom follow her in the door. "What smells so good?" they ask. Michelle hears them talking and wakes up. Michael says, "I made tomato sauce. Grandpa Frank helped me; Grandpa Frank, Annabelle, Michelle, and I will make pizza."

"Kitchen crew, put your aprons on, wash your hands, and let us begin. We will double the recipe because we need more than one pizza." Mom and Dad shake their heads and wish them luck. Grandpa Frank laughs and says, "We are professional pizza makers. Wait and see how good these pizzas taste." He turns to Annabelle, Michael, and Michelle. "Annabelle, measure one cup of warm water. Make sure it is warm, not hot or cold. It has to be perfect. Michelle, you open the packet of yeast, and Michael, you sprinkle the yeast over the water and wait about 5 minutes. Let me help you with these measurements. We add one-fourth tsp salt and one-fourth tsp sugar and wait until it bubbles a little. Add two tsp of olive oil to the water and wait. Michelle, measure three cups of flour. This part gets tricky. Annabelle, add the flour to the water and mix; if it is too sticky, add a little more flour. Michelle and Michael put flour on the board your dad uses for piecrusts. Here we go. Annabelle, place the dough on the floured board and form a big ball like a basketball. Make sure it is not sticky. Add a little more flour if needed. Michelle, you punch it about four times. Michael, turn the dough over and punch it some more.

Annabelle, shape it into a round ball. We will let it sit there for about ½ hour. We can shred the mozzarella cheese and prepare the toppings while waiting. Michael and Michelle, bring the rolling pin. You will take turns rolling the dough out to fit the pans."

Michael says, "I want to throw it up in the air and try to catch it. I saw someone do that in the movies once." Grandpa tells him, "I see things in the movies, too. They are not always real. You can try it another time, not today." We are ready for the topping. "Annabelle, you set the oven at four hundred. MICHAEL, WITH AN IMPISH GRIN ON HIS FACE, HAS THE PIZZA DOUGH IN HIS HANDS READY TO LET IT FLY. "Michael, Grandpa Frank told you, NOT NOW. You must listen." "I know I can do it right. I must try," Michael insists. He rolls it out, takes it, swirls it, and tosses it up in the air. It flew and landed on the sailing and stuck. Grandpa Frank looks at Michael and says, "You are a wonder. It is good to want and try things, but not when other people are involved. You must listen to the grown-up people in charge. No one wants you or someone else to get hurt. Grandpa looks up just as the dough is falling. It lands right on his head. Michael stands with a look of surprise. Grandpa is standing with pizza dough hanging from his chin, ears, and hair. Michael thinks, "Oh no, what did I do? This is not good." Grandpa, being grandpa, takes the dough and places it on the table, except for the parts in his hair on top of his head. "Michael, when will you listen? This way, I know you will own a pizza parlor one day, but for now, get this dough away from my head."

Michael nods quietly. "Michael, let this be a tasty lesson. Your pizza is on my head, but let's make some more," Grandpa laughs as Michael cleans the mess. As only a grandpa can do, he laughs as they start anew. Grandpa continues, "Now, help me spread the cheese on the dough so we can have pizza. We are going to put the cheese on first. This is our professional secret. Do you want sausage, pepperoni, broccoli, or something else? Decide now because once we put the tomato sauce on and more cheese, it goes in the oven for about twenty minutes. Michelle, set the table and call Mom and Dad for pizza." As

Grandpa Frank finishes, Annabelle asks, "Grandpa, why is Wisdom a gift?"

"What brought that question up right now?" "I was thinking of Father Murphy and Michael."

"It means that we show our love for God by doing the right thing. What we want is not always the right thing to do," I happily intervene. Grandpa Frank agrees, "Sounds right to me." He turns to Michael. "Michael, what are you doing? Oh, no, you could not have dropped the flour on top of the pizza. Did you?" Michael smiles and says, "Fooled you. It did fall, all by itself. I was only trying to put it away when it jumped out of my hands and fell on the table right next to the pizza." "Michael, Michael, flour cannot jump out of your hands. It is okay to say you dropped it. We know you were trying to help."

The pizza is good, but Annabelle is in a rush. After dinner, she searches for information about St. Eulalia for her Confirmation class. Grandpa Frank is busy killing flies. The fly swatter is raised high as Grandpa Frank swoops right toward the fly. He moves fast, but the fly moves faster. Grandpa Frank is determined. He raises the fly swatter again. He looks up, looks down, and wham. He gets her. Grandpa Frank carries the fly to the backyard. The fly is gone. "Michael and Michelle, do you want to go fishing tomorrow?"

"Can Marcus come too?" Michael asks excitedly. "Of course, he can," says Grandpa Frank. Marcus is so excited. He has never been fishing. This is going to be his first time. "Can Willie come too?" Willie, Marcus's pet dog, barks loudly as he hears the news. Flossie, our pet pony, hears Marcus and Willie and wakes up, ready to join them. Grandpa Frank says, "Of course, they can come; Willie and Flossie might catch more fish than we do."

THE BAIT

Grandpa Frank, Michael, Marcus, Flossie, and Willie are walking towards the lake. The lake is about one and a half miles from their house. Grandpa Frank is carrying his fishing pole. Flossie and Willie are bringing lunch and water on their backs. Michael and Marcus have the bait and their fishing poles. They have fishing hats on their heads. Flossie has been helping Uncle Joe on the farm for two weeks and is happy to relax. Willie wants to go swimming, but Grandpa Frank told him, "Not yet." He explains all that noise would scare the fish away. Grandpa Frank is helping Michael and Marcus with their fishing poles when Michelle starts crying.

"What's wrong?" asks Grandpa Frank. "I was thinking of Eulalia. Annabelle told me about her. Eulalia was martyred and was the same age as Annabelle. I do not think I can be that brave." Grandpa Frank says, "Not to worry. You are braver than you know. Eulalia was one of the saints who suffered for her faith. God gives certain people special graces and strength to endure trials of pain. No one likes pain, but we offer it up to help others. Besides, why are you sad? Saint Eulalia is in Heaven. She is happy and wants you to be happy. Let's get the bait and catch a fish."

Michelle cast her line, followed by Michael and Marcus. Marcus needs help. His fishing line gets tangled in Flossie's tail. Willie starts barking when Michelle calls out, "I caught something. I hope it is a fish." Grandpa Frank looks around and wades out to Michelle. "Reel your line like I showed you. Sure enough, a fish is dangling from the end of the line." Grandpa Frank looks at Michelle and says, "He is small; I think you should let him go." Michelle cut him loose. She feels good. At least she caught something. Grandpa Frank and Michael help Marcus untangle his line from Flossie's tail. Marcus is finally able to try fishing and joins Michael at the edge of the water. Marcus feels a tug in his line, and Grandpa Frank is there to help him. Marcus is so excited that he almost drops his fishing pole but hangs on. He has a gigantic fish on his line. He struggles. Grandpa Frank is laughing as the fish fights to be free, but Marcus hangs on, and with Grandpa Frank's help, the fish becomes his first catch. Willie, Marcus's pet dog, jumps in and lands on top of Marcus. Marcus drops his fish and watches it swim away. Marcus does not know what to do until Grandpa Frank starts to laugh. Marcus does not think this is the least bit funny, but when Willie climbs out of the water, Marcus has to join them in laughing for the entire day.

Flossie wakes up as they are getting ready to walk home. She had slept the whole afternoon except for her sore tail. Grandpa Frank tells her, "You worked too long and hard these past two weeks. You need a vacation from the farm for a while." As they walk home, they still laugh at all that happened to them. Mom and Dad are working. Annabelle is in her confirmation class. Confirmation is next week. She is teaching us everything she learned about the gift of wisdom. Michael says, "I am not old enough for that gift." Grandpa Frank laughs and says, "O, Michael, you are more than old enough. Wisdom is using your knowledge to choose the difference between what is right and what is wrong. Michael, you did that today. You invited your friend, Marcus, to come with us. You helped him with his fishing line and taught him how to fish. You do your best to listen to your mom and dad and help Annabelle take care of Flossie. Everything you do that is good and right makes God happy."

"I am old enough, but there is so much more to learn," says Michael sadly. "You got that right," says Grandpa Frank. I see him smiling.

DATE TO REMEMBER

Michel, Michelle, and Annabelle are having fun playing with our pet pony—Flossie.

I, Aunt Bess, am reading "Lord of the Flies." No wonder Annabelle likes to read so much. We both always have a book in our hands. Today, we are going to the movies, which is unusual. Their mom and dad do not like many movies. They always tell their children, "They are inappropriate for you to see, just a waste of time and money." They are right. They usually are. St. Joseph's School is having a fundraiser and is showing "Sound of Music." "The Parent's Guild" sells popcorn and all kinds of things for people to buy. It should be fun. My sister, Helen, and I are going also. It is one of our favorite movies. Michael should like it. He will enjoy the popcorn even if he does not understand the movie.

Their dad, is doing work around the garden. Flossie is helping him. He pulls out the weeds, and Flossie picks them up and puts them in one big pile. Dad puts on music and sings while he works. He sometimes likes being by himself; he says he is never alone. We all need quiet time to think about life. After the movie and popcorn, we decide to walk home. John promised us barbecued chicken tonight with a tossed salad. He cooks when mom must work late or does something special with us. He is a good cook.

Desserts are his favorite food. Sometimes, dinner is better when Dad cooks, especially for Michael, but they better not say anything; otherwise, they will wind up cooking for themselves.

Marcus, Michael's new friend and neighbor, waits for Michael when we arrive home; he has cream all over his face and arms. "What happened?" We ask at the same time. "I am itchy," Marcus replies. "The yard is filled with poison ivy. We did not know what it was, so we pulled it up without gloves. Wait until you see my mom and dad. We went to the hospital." My sister (Michael's mom) went right over to their house. She met Marcus' mom at their back door. "How can I help you? This is terrible. Where are your clothes? They must be washed, and everything you wear or touch. Let me go home, get a pair of gloves and a big plastic bag to put them in. Poison ivy spreads easily. I will wash everything, even your sneakers. What about Willie?"

"Can you believe? Willie is a smart dog. He would not come near us while we were weeding. He still will not come near us. We frightened him away. We do look scary with all this cream on us."

"If you would like, we can keep Willie at our house. If he catches this rash from you, he will be a mess. Show us where the poison ivy is growing, and we will kill it for you."

"We did not know it was poison ivy. Now we do. We will always know. At the hospital, they told us, leaves of three, let it be. They told us that was a good general way to avoid poisonous plants."

"Good idea," says Mom. "Let's deal with the poison ivy clothes. I will wash them for you and your sneakers, and then we will bring you supper and kill the weeds."

"How do you kill them? We thought you could pull them out."

"You can, but you must kill the root. Weeds thrive in hundreds of places. We need one cup of salt, one gallon of white vinegar, and eight to ten cups of dish detergent water. We will pour it on. Your yard has a big amount of poison ivy."

We do not want anyone to become infected with poison ivy. My sister took charge. She does not let anyone touch the clothing, but I, Aunt Bess, oversaw the salt and vinegar. Michelle and Michael bring Willie to Flossie's house, where the two of them like the idea of being together. Our family is always ready to help, especially in an emergency. Annabelle and her mother have everything under control. They bring over cold iced tea and a big salad for Marcus and his mom and dad. My sister is known for her salads. They are loaded with cheese, chicken, tomatoes, and peppers. I am thinking about all my family is doing to help our neighbors. My family is doing service without even thinking about it. A neighbor needs help, and we help.

Mom, Annabelle, Michelle, and Michael are looking forward to one of Dad's desserts, Blueberry pie with ice cream. I join them for dessert. Annabelle and Michelle have been helping Marcus' mom and dad clean up their kitchen. They also get Willie's dishes for food and water. I turn to Annabelle and say, "I have something serious to tell you." I have been thinking and praying about this for a long time. I will tell everyone after dinner what my hopes and plans are, God willing, for the future.

Annabelle asks, "Aunt Bess, what will you tell us?"

"I always felt a desire to help others. I have been spending time pondering this idea. Some organizations help young adults. Covenant House in New York City helps children in challenging situations. Life Choices allows mothers and their babies. Two compassionate, faith-filled women started this program. I always admired them, and I want to be like them. I will go where the need is the greatest."

Michelle asked, "Can I help, too?"

"Yes, but in a unique way. You can help take care of Michael. He is almost six, and you are eight. That is an enormous difference. You also can let your hair grow long and have it cut so it can become a wig for children who lose their hair when they are sick."

"Annabelle, you should start thinking of ways you can help," I say. Mom asked, "Where will you be staying?"

"Good question. I am not sure yet. I have requested information from four places and am waiting for an answer. You will be the first to know." Annabelle has a sad reaction. "We are going to miss you." Michael starts to cry. "What is wrong? This is good news. Life will be different but better. New experiences are exciting. Michael, come over here; we need a hug. Be happy."

"Let's make this a day to remember and have a second helping of our special dessert. Things always work out according to God's plan." Annabelle asks me, "Aunt Bess, how did she know?"

"This is what God wants her to do," I tell her about how she always feels the need to help others. I tell Annabelle how I helped at Walburga's Orphanage in Roselle when I was her age. "It was a German order of nuns who cared for babies to live in home and little children. They save the lives of babies. All the children wanted was to be held, nothing else. They needed the comfort and security of my arms holding them. It was unfortunate when the nuns had to sell the building. Roselle Catholic High School has been there for many years since then."

"We all must continue doing what is right. We do our best to manage the rest with God's help. New babies and mothers must know there are arms to hug and help them. Promise me that you will pray for me every night. I need your prayers. We need God's help in everything we hope to accomplish in this life." We finish the blueberry pie and give hugs as we make our way to bed for the night. I remind everyone that the love we share as a family gives us strength to bring joy and comfort to others. The children wake up to a new day with me, their Aunt Bess. Mom and Dad smile as we are told the good news. I will not be traveling. I will live here with my family and work in New Jersey. Michael jumps up and gives me a big hug. Flossie and Willie stand by the door, waiting for a hug from Michael. Those two always need hugs, especially from Michael. This is a day to remember!

DO NOT JUMP

Being her favorite, I, Aunt Bess, am telling Annabelle that this is not a clever idea. Annabelle thinks her ideas are always good. This time, she is not too sure. At first, it sounded fun, but she is frightened by the prospect of jumping out of a plane. Annabelle, usually a level-headed, mature thirteen-year-old, thought it would be fun to go skydiving, but now, her stomach is doing flip-flops. She is thinking, "Why would anyone in their right mind jump out of a plane?" Michelle, eight years old with curly brown hair, looks out the plane window and asks, "Are we safe?" Michael, an adventurous five-year-old, is sitting next to her. Suddenly, Annabelle hears a loud voice, "Annabelle, wake Michael and Michelle; we are running late. It is time to leave."

***

I wake up and think I must have been dreaming, or was I having a nightmare? "Annabelle, ask Aunt Bess to help you. We are late to pick up your father. We are going to Sky Manor Airport, in Pittstown. It is about a two-hour drive, and we do not want to be late. Let's move." On the way to the airport, I, Aunt Bess, tell everyone about my dream. It was surreal. I can still see Michelle looking out the window and Michael sitting beside her. Annabelle tells them that skydiving is on her bucket list, a list of "to-do things" in life. She even wants to skydive with Flossie. Mom laughs. "You are too young, and Flossie cannot jump from a plane. That is something no pony should ever do." I think our family pet, Flossie, agrees with that statement. Dad John is waiting and sees us before we see him. After many hugs and kisses, we pile back into the van. Mom starts telling Dad about my dream and how Annabelle wants to sky-dive. Dad says, "Annabelle, look out the window, and you can see what you would look like up in the air."

Annabelle looks thoughtful and says, "Maybe next year." Michael is looking and listening to all this conversation. He is quiet for now, but he never stops listening and thinking.

"It looks like fun," says Michael. Michelle says, "Aunt Bess, it looks fun, but you better know what you are doing. They have classes to teach you the right way to sky-dive. Nothing is ever as simple as it looks." Mom starts talking about Dad's trip and how we missed him. Dad is explaining the importance of his work project and how glad he is to be back home. Dad begins his conversation with Annabelle. "If you are still interested in a new adventure next year, you must prepare for that adventure. You must read, learn what is involved, and save money for lessons and enough to pay for your adventure. Then you will be mature enough to try it."

Annabelle is happy with that thought. Dad is thinking of a big grilled cheeseburger with two pickles on top. Mom gets busy in the kitchen while Michelle helps me fix the table. Annabelle is making a special dessert—ice cream; it is the easiest.

There is a slight noise, like someone scratching a wall. I look around and do not see anything. I look up and see Michael. He is wrapped in a sheet, climbing out the third-floor window. Michael is going to sky-dive without a parachute. (He thinks). Dad runs inside and is on the third floor in seconds. Mom calls the fire department, Flossie jumps to her feet, Annabelle grabs the ladder, and Michelle, bewildered by all this commotion, starts to cry. I freeze; Michael stands there, wrapped in a sheet. Dad says, "Michael, do not jump, at least not yet. We better talk just a bit. Remember the St. Michael prayer you learned this year? We will say it together while you climb back in the window. He will help you stay safe. Say it with me. 'St. Michael, the Archangel, defends us in battle. Be our protection against the wickedness and snares of the devil. May God rebuke him, we humbly pray, and so thousand do thou, O prince of the Heavenly Hosts, by the power of God, thrust into hell Satan and all the evil spirits who prowl about the world seeking the ruin of all souls.' Amen."

Michael says the prayer with Dad but does not move. He tells Dad, "I am scared. This is not a clever idea." While they are praying the St.

Michael prayer, Annabelle and Mom set up the ladder, and Flossie is trying to climb the steps of the ladder. This is not an easy feat for a pony. The firefighters arrive, and Michael looks at all the commotion. He sees Michelle crying, Mom collapsed in a chair, and me still frozen in fear. And Dad, still strong, tells Michael to keep his eyes open and repeat what he says, "St. Michael, help me take one step at a time. Help me get back inside." Michael does just that. He slowly takes one step after another. He is at the window. He stretches out his arms to grab Dad, loses his balance, and falls right into his father's arms. The firefighters are on the roof when Michael falls into his father's arms. Mom stands up and prays loudly, "Thank You, God!" Michelle smiles, Annabelle feels relieved, and I defrost.

Michael, back on solid ground, receives a full-blown lecture from Dad. He reads the riot act and listens carefully while Dad explains of all the dangers. Reminding him, "Michael's way is not always the right way unless you happen to be an angel!"

The day came to a successful conclusion. Dad has his cheeseburger; the firefighters have one also, and Flossie receives a particular fireman's hat for attempted bravery. Annabelle also learns that it is best to explain fully to Michael the dangers of new adventures without preparation. We thank God for a special day—Dad is home, Michael is safe, and we are together.

ONE WORD

"Think about it."

Annabelle, at age thirteen, thinks a lot. Annabelle is thinking and hoping for a beautiful Easter Sunday. She wants everyone to enjoy the day. Michelle, her eight-year-old sister, and Michael, her little brother, aged five, are excited about Easter. She knows the "Easter Bunny" will come for Michael. Dad will have a corsage for Mom, Michelle, Annabelle, and me, Aunt Bess. I, Aunt Bess, have become a second mother to my sister's children. When she needed help, I helped her. She still needs help, so here I am. Michael, almost six, will wear his new suit. We will all go to church on Easter. Annabelle hopes Mom is planning a big Easter dinner with her uncles, aunts, and cousins. It is always fun when family and special friends get together, especially for a holiday. Michelle, eight years old with long curly hair, is smiling. Annabelle thinks to herself, "I wonder what Michelle is thinking?" Michelle says, "I would like an Easter bonnet." Annabelle starts to laugh. "No one wears an Easter bonnet anymore." I tell her, "Michelle will do what she knows is proper. Since when have you been worried about what other people think and do? You must always do what is right, and you will never have to worry if you are with God. Now, I do not think God is worried about an Easter bonnet, but if you feel a hat shows respect and grandeur, then wear one, at least to church."

Michael is looking for flowers. I suggest, "Let's go on a shopping expedition. Michael, we will help you decorate later." Shopping for a new hat is quite an experience, especially for Michelle. We go to seventeen stores. Finally, Michelle tried on a hat with yellow and red flowers on the brim. It is beautiful. She looks like a flowerpot, but she is happy. Next, she wants to help with the Easter Egg hunt. I, Aunt Bess, school her, "Michelle, you are rushing. The days before Easter are important Holy days. Without them, there would be no Easter. Did you forget why we celebrate Easter Sunday? Our Lord rose from the dead. Remember how he suffered for us and our sins. He did all this for us so that someday we can be in Heaven with Him. This is why we try to live by all the rules or commandments He gave us. It always makes us feel good when we do not break any of those rules." Michael just looks at us and thinks to himself, "I wonder if that is always true." But Michael is only five and has only broken a tiny bit of rules. He knows he is not supposed to go into the cookie jar, but those cookies taste so good. Michael also knows that he better not leave the yard by himself. It seems as if rules can be broken. I heard that someplace, but I do not think it is a good idea. We can never break God's rules. But our rules are different. If we do not think the rules are good, we should help change them.

I ask, "Michael, what are you thinking? Whatever it is, do not do it. Annabelle and Michelle, come help us. We are going to help Michael decorate our house for Easter."

"When are we going to color the eggs, and why do we color eggs?" asks Michael. "We will color them on Saturday, the day before Sunday, so they look pretty. It is a little more than that, but that is good reason for now."

"Mom, I cut myself. I am bleeding," says Michelle. "That is only a little cut on your finger. What are you trying to do?" Mom asks calmly. Michelle answered, "I am trying to make a paper flower. It will look pretty on the table."

"Yes. It will, and that is where it will go. Do you know what? Michelle, you did something for your family out of love; you cut yourself and started to bleed. That is the same idea as what Jesus did for us. Jesus bled heavily, more than your finger. That is one of the reasons we dye our eggs red. To remind us of the love that Jesus has for all of us." Just at that moment, the phone rang. Michael picks it up and says, "Hello." Mom asks, "Who is it?" "It's Uncle Joe, and he wants to talk to you."

"Beth and I think it would be fun if you could come here for Easter," says Uncle Joe. "Let me talk to my brother Joe." Mom takes the phone. "Tell Michael the Easter bunny lives near the farm and often visits here," says Uncle Joe. "Joe, it is important that you all come for Easter. Just trust me." Dad looks at Mom as she talks to Uncle Joe, and he shakes his head. Now, we will all be at Uncle Joe's for Easter. Uncle Joe invites all our uncles, aunts, and cousins for Easter dinner. They all live on farms near Uncle Joe's. We have to drive about three hours to the farm in Pennsylvania. Uncle Joe and Aunt Beth want us there by Wednesday for all the church services. Annabelle is trying to explain to Michelle and Michael why the three days before Easter are so important. Suddenly, Michelle interrupts Annabelle. Her new Easter hat is missing, and she cannot go anywhere without it. The search begins. Annabelle looks at Michelle and says, "You are wearing it." Annabelle ended her explanation (for now).

Holy Week is important. Tomorrow is Palm Sunday, and we are having a procession holding palms. Monday and Tuesday are busy. Mom decides it is spring cleaning time. She wants everything nice and new for Easter. She says even if we are at Uncle Joe's, it will be nice when we return. Wednesday finally arrives. Mom has carefully packed all the food in coolers and bags, plus we each have suitcases for our own stuff like clothes and shoes. Good thing we have a big van. We leave early in the morning. Michael, Michelle, Annabelle, and I are sitting together, and I am telling the story of Peter Rabbit.

"He would try and take half the vegetables from his neighbor's garden. Peter Rabbit would always get caught. Once, Peter even ran away. Peter reminds me a little of Michael. (I hope Michael did not hear about how Peter ran away. Michael does not need any innovative ideas). Annabelle tells us about today and why it is important. "If you have a friend or someone you love who is extremely sick and you leave them to suffer alone, that is just what the friends of Jesus did. They left Jesus to suffer alone after Judas betrayed Him."

"We're at Uncle Joe's," calls out dad.

"Who is Judas?" asks Michelle. "Later," says Annabelle.

Aunt Beth and Uncle Joe come right out to help us unpack. We have supper and off to church. We do learn about Judas and how he betrayed his friend, Jesus. But we also learn that no matter how tough life can be, Jesus will never leave us alone. Tomorrow, Uncle Joe and Dad are having their feet washed. "Why would they do that?" asks Michelle. "Do you remember last summer when you wore sandals? Your feet got sandy and dusty when you were outside? Back then, everyone wore sandals and had dusty feet. They always washed them before they sat down for dinner. Jesus washed their feet to show His love and humility for humankind. It is called Holy Thursday, the Last Supper."

"Aunt Bess, when are we going to color the eggs?" asks Michael. "I am tired of church." I start to laugh. "Michael, you are not tired of church. You are tired of us talking so much, and I do not blame you. I am tired of us talking so much, too. Let us get busy now, but Michael, if we did not have the church, there would be no reason to ever celebrate any holiday. Think about that for a while. You will understand more next year. We will make the eggs on Saturday, but we can make Easter bread tomorrow. Let's all get a good night's sleep."

Uncle Joe chimes in, "Tomorrow, we will be busy. Sleep well."

Michael wakes up and walks to the kitchen. He quietly opens the refrigerator door. He stands there and looks inside. "That is six dozen eggs," he thinks to himself. "I should not do this." Michael keeps staring at all the eggs. He hears someone moving in the next room. "I better not touch those eggs, at least by myself." At that moment, Aunt Beth walks into the kitchen. "Michael, what are you doing? I hope you did not touch the eggs?"

"Oh, no," says Michael to himself. "That was a close call."

"I am glad you are here. You can help us make Easter bread. Michael, we need at least two dozen eggs to be colored." Aunt Beth reminds him it is more fun when we do this together. Aunt Beth,

Annabelle, and Michelle are kneading the bread. Aunt Beth and all of us make four loaves of Easter bread. We help clean the kitchen while Dad and Uncle Joe get ready for church. They make sure their feet are clean before the washing of the feet. Aunt Beth, Michelle, Michael, Annabelle, and I dress for church, and we all leave in the van. Michael falls asleep, but we all listen closely as Father Murphy explains that God was bending down to us because of His total love for us. We must be more like Jesus to show our love for others. "That is not always easy," Annabelle thinks.

Tomorrow is "Good Friday." Michelle asks why it is called "Good Friday." "It is the day Jesus died," her dad tells her. "Evil people put Jesus to death. I do not think anyone thought it was good until Sunday. In three days, Jesus rose from the dead and showed the world His love. He suffered and died for us. He put His whole trust in God, the Father, which is what we must do. Despite the terrible things people do, we must trust God to help us do the right thing." We arrive at church and hear the story of Jesus. It was sad.

Finally, Saturday arrives, and Aunt Beth takes charge. She always does, and that is a good thing. Aunt Beth is a top-notch organizer. (She worked for Toys R Us… They must organize all those shelves). The eggs are hard-boiled, cooled, and ready to be colored and decorated. Aunt Beth gives us each six eggs and says, "Be creative." Michelle is helping Michael draw flowers and crosses and adding names on each egg. They have one for everyone. Aunt Beth, Mom, Dad, Aunt Bess (me), and Uncle Joe show up just in time to hide the eggs. Their cousins would never find them. Annabelle hides hers up a tree. Michelle would not tell anyone where she hid hers. Mom, Dad, Aunt Beth, and Uncle Joe say they would hide theirs later. There is a knock on the door—flowers, a white gardenia for Mom, Aunt Beth, Michelle, Annabelle, and me.

Easter Sunday and we are going to celebrate. The church is all about the Resurrection of Jesus. We learn how to look for the face of Jesus in every person we meet and put our trust in God. After church, the rest of our family comes for breakfast and the Easter egg hunt. We have our Easter bread with something hot to drink, and the hunt begins. Greg finds one dozen; Frank finds the same. That is twenty-four. There are twenty-four more eggs to find. Gianna runs up. She has ten eggs in her basket—fourteen more. Mary Claire finds two in the straw. Julia sees the tree; six more are found—eighteen more to go. Conner finds one; five more to go. Along comes Joey with Annie and the last five. The hunt is a success.

As we come to the end of our Easter celebration, Uncle Joe says, "I have something serious to tell all of you. Aunt Beth and I are not blessed with children of our own, but we are blessed to have you as our family. We love all of you. We are not sick or dying now. We want to make sure the farm stays in our family. Aunt Beth and I have spent hours telling you about your family this past year. It is important to maintain that spirit of togetherness. Life is truly short. We are here to help each other overcome the loneliness and conflicts of this world. The lies and deceptions that exist can be overcome with prayer, demanding work, and perseverance. Remember the past and learn from it; do not relive it. History is knowledge. Learn from it. Do not make the same mistakes. Make new ones. Right this minute, we want to make sure all of you know we are leaving a legacy of history to my brother and his family. We want to leave the farm for my brother, John, his wife, Helen, and their children. This way, it will stay in our family, and you will continue to live near each other. We want everyone to know exactly what our hopes are for the future of the farm. We have been teaching my brother and your cousins how to work on the farm and care for the animals. It only takes one word. We want all of you to know our hopes."

"What is the word?" Michael asks. "WOW!"

A big cheer is heard with a resounding "YES!"

After that big announcement, we give each other hugs and smiles. Uncle Joe and Aunt Beth are already planning our next celebration.

PRAY, WORK, PERSEVERE

Are you ready for another story?

In case you haven't heard my previous stories, I am Aunt Bess. Annabelle's mother, Helen, is my sister. My hair is brown with a tinge of gray. I am a storyteller at heart, finding joy in life through the company of children. As you may have realized, life is an adventure, particularly involving children and their pony, Flossie. Children keep me young, especially Michael. He has so many questions.

"Aunt Bess, why is today so special?" asks Michael.

"Every day is special, especially when you are here. June 30th is the last day before the July 4th weekend. All true Americans celebrate July 4th. It should remind us of all the work and wars that our ancestors went through so that we can have opportunities to succeed in this life. They showed us that we can succeed if we pray, work hard, and persevere."

June 30th also reminds us that summer goes quickly. We must have a smile every day. "Today is an ice cream soda day," says Michelle, an eight-year-old girl with curly brown hair, and Annabelle, thirteen years old and Michael's big sister. She does like to read and wears black-framed glasses. "Does Flossie know today is ice cream soda day?" I ask. "Not yet, but she will," comes a chorus of voices. "Ice cream for all," says Mom.

"This sounds like a real treat. You too, Flossie. Your favorite, vanilla fudge. There is soda if you want to be authentic."

"Now is a suitable time to think about this weekend and our summer plans," said Mom and Dad.

"Dad, will you build us a tree house?" asks Michael. "Annabelle can read, Michelle can brush her hair, and I can eat chocolate chip cookies. You and Mom can come too. Maybe Aunt Bess, if she can climb up there. Aunt Bess says she is almost thirty, but that is old. I do not think Flossie will fit, but she can try."

"You know what," Michael says. "If everyone helps, we can build it together. It is an innovative idea and sounds like fun." Mom says, "Ask your cousin, Amanda, if she has time to help us. She can make the blueprints for us to do it right. This will be the biggest and best tree house ever built." Mom and Dad say, "Promising idea, Michael. Your cousin is a creative, talented architect." Michelle says, "She's funny and makes me laugh."

"Does anyone else have plans?" asks Dad. "Uncle Joe has invited us back to the farm for a visit this summer," Mom says, "This is more than enough for one summer. Time goes fast when you are having fun. This month, in July, we can focus on the tree house, and in August, we can visit Uncle Joe."

"Annabelle, did you call Amanda about the tree house?"

"I am on the phone right now. It is more complicated than we thought," Annabelle says. "About two weeks," Dad says. "We should do it right so we can all enjoy spending time in our tree house. This might take us all summer, but it will be fun. When we finish, we will invite Uncle Joe and Aunt Beth to a tree house party."

"Michael, you can help me pick the best tree. We must make a list of all the materials we will need. July is going to be a busy month. I have a feeling August will be busy, also." We need a permit. I am unsure, but I ask Mom to call City Hall to find out if we need a building permit. Flossie is sad. She feels left out of all the summer plans. Flossie, as you know, is our family pet, a brown pony with a big heart who loves ginger cookies. I see her and speak to her gently, "Flossie, we cannot do any of this without you. You must help us carry the lumber, and you know Michael. Anything is possible." I have learned to use the word hope instead of plan. "We hope to build a treehouse this summer with your help."

Michael runs in, all excited. "Look at what I found."

"Michael, it is a baby bird. It must have fallen out of its nest. Where did you find the baby bird?"

"Right by the tree we were looking at for our tree house."

"We must find her nest. It is a good thing that the blueprints take time. By then, this little bird will be ready to fly on her own. And we will still be able to build in this tree."

"Can I give her a name?" asks Michael.

"Of course."

"Can I call her Tumble?"

"That's a funny name," I say.

"No, it is not. Mom says I tumble every time I fall. This baby bird fell, so she took a tumble."

"You are right. We will call her Tumble. Now, let's put her back in her nest."

"Michael, Michelle, Annabelle, come over here," calls Dad. "We must sit down and make a list of what we need for our tree house."

"We have tools and a ladder already, but we need wood and nails. Tape measure, level, square, and we better check with Amanda. We will need a roof and windows, which is getting more complicated than I thought." Dad is thinking, "What did I get myself into?" Michael is thinking, "This is exciting." Michelle thinks, "I can brush my hair up in the sky, and maybe it will become straight." I whisper to myself, "No one seems to know what they are doing." Mom just offers a silent prayer that no one gets hurt. Dad takes out a notebook and starts to make a list. "First, we must make sure the tree is big and sturdy enough to build a tree house in it. The one Michael and I chose is good, but we all must agree. Second, we need two hammers. Third, we need a rope because it will be fun to use a rope to climb into the tree house. We will have some kind of stairs, but a rope is intriguing. We will have both. Fourth, we have to measure the height. It should be about six feet high. Michael is not that tall yet, and if he falls, he will not be that far from the ground. That is true in case anyone trips or falls. That will not happen, but it is always best to hope for the best and prepare for the worst ahead of time. Annabelle, do research and see what else we need. We cannot get the lumber until we see the blueprints."

Listening to all this conversation, I ask, "How will you furnish your tree house?" It was just a thought for conversation.

Michael says, "I need a bed. I want to sleep in it at night." Mom says, "No bed." Dad says, "We will see about that. If it happens, use a sleeping bag as if you are camping. It is the same thing, except you will not be on the ground." Speaking loudly, I chip in, "We better build it first. Then decide about sleeping."

"You cannot sleep out here alone. I like my bed, so count me out; Mom and Dad would never let you sleep outside in the dark alone," says Annabelle. Annabelle completed her research and gave the list to Dad. "Annabelle, Are you sure we need all of this?" asks Dad. "What have I done?" thinks Dad. "I am going to lose my mind." Michael smiles, and Michelle is happy. Dad decides, "This is worth the work."

The doorbell rings. Special delivery. The blueprints have arrived. Dad and Mom spend the next hour or so looking at the blueprints and shaking their heads. They finally look up and say, "Aunt Amanda is incredibly detailed, and her thinking is way beyond our ideas. We need help. Let me call Uncle Joe. He built his barn and might be able to help." After a lengthy conversation with Uncle Joe, Dad turns to us and says, "We are good to go. Uncle Joe will help us, as he has lumber we can use; plus, he reminded me of all our cousins. They want to be a part of this project. This is going to be some tree house!"

July came, and so did Uncle Joe, along with a good friend of his who happened to be a retired carpenter. Dad is overwhelmed. Mom is confused, and Michael is happy. Uncle Joe and his friend, Marvin, look over the blueprints and say, "No problem." Dad shakes his head.

Mom is amazed. Michael smiles. Our project begins. Marvin says, "We should make it 5 ft. That seems like a good height for Michael and Michelle. We will decide as we progress. Let us all sit down and organize exactly how we are going to build this tree house. First, you have a good tree. It is a big, sturdy oak with strong branches. You have the blueprints. We must figure out how much wood and supplies we need. We get them and begin. Uncle Joe and his friend, Marvin, begin cutting and hammering. Soon, the foundation will be built. Tumble had flown out of his nest a few days ago. So, we can safely start building in the tree."

Suddenly, there was a booming noise that caused everyone to jump. Marvin drops his hammer, and Dad nearly cuts the wood in half. All the cousins have arrived with enough food for a giant barbecue. Party Time! They all came to help, but they sure are not going to starve while they work. Marvin is in charge. He breaks everyone into groups with different responsibilities. He oversees all the groups. Dad and my cousins, Paul and Peter, will lay out the platform. Denise, Katherine, Joan, and Susan will help with the walls. Marvin will be busy helping them attach the walls to the floor. That part looks like you better know what you are doing.

Marvin, Dad, and Mom said, "That is enough work for one day. Let us enjoy our meal together." Michael announces, "We should pray. 'Thank you, God, for this special day'."

The next day came sooner than expected. Uncle Joe and Marvin are right here to begin another day's work. I think we will be finished before August. Marvin begins cutting wood and nailing boards together. He is waiting for us to help him complete the framing of our tree house. And just to let them know she is here, Annabelle yells out, "Here I am. Uncle Joe, Marvin, how can I help?"

"Grab a hammer, and I will show you," says Dad. He showed up just in time. The more hands, the better. The framing of the walls was complete and up went the walls. Uncle Joe, Marvin, and Dad are working on the roof. Marvin tells Dad that his friend Bill was coming over to cut out the windows and doors after he framed them. Michelle decided flower boxes would be underneath the windows. She is filling them with dirt and deciding on the flowers that would look nice. The only problem is they would not get enough sun. There must be a flower that does not need sun. She has to research that problem. Flossie is watching all this activity from her house, our two-car heated garage. She is sad. She thinks they forgot about her until Michelle says, "Flossie, come over here. We need to see how tall you are so we can build the right height. You have to be able to stand under our tree house." Greg, our cousin, has the best idea. He wants Uncle Joe to build a special platform underneath our tree house. "You can stand or sleep right by us, Flossie. Our tree house will be six feet off the ground, not five feet. Greg wants to make sure you have enough room to stretch and be comfortable. Your platform will go around the whole tree."

Greg also helps Michelle with her flower boxes. He suggests that instead of trying to find flowers that grow without sun, fill the boxes with white sand or gravel and put the United States flags in them. They make small flags so she could put a few in each box. We can have a big flag right by the door of our tree house. We begin building it close to July 4th. The flags are a good reminder that we still have the freedom to think for ourselves.

Dad is yelling, "Joe, come here. I need your help." Uncle Joe looks up and says loudly, "You cannot do that by yourself. Marvin has a friend who is coming to help with the roof. His name is Anthony, and he is a roofer. He will help us do it right. We can finish the trim and handrails for the stairs after the roof is finished, which will be tomorrow. That is enough for today." Mom, Aunt Beth, and I have been working all day preparing a huge pot of chili, salad, garlic rolls, and chips, plus a surprise dessert. There is a moment or two of silence as we all collapse from a good but hard day's work. We looked at the almost completed tree house and agreed it looked good. Dad thinks to himself, "We should be completed in two more days. We must have our tree house blessed and pray we enjoy having fun without mishaps. How will I arrange this?"

I am thinking aloud, "I have an idea but need your help." I begin organizing the entire evening in my head. *We will have a tree house party and invite our friends, including Father Murphy, Rabbi Eugene, and Pastor Smith, to our guest list. Mom Helen calls to ask them to join our celebration. She tells them Dad John would like their blessings on our project, the family tree house. The tree house is completed in three weeks, not four. Even Flossie's platform is done, the window boxes with flags, the big flag, and the rope to climb. Party Time!*

After Father Murphy, Rabbi Eugene, and Pastor Smith invoked the blessings of God upon us and our tree house, we celebrated. I, with the help of family members, arranged a spectacular feast. Flossie came to be part of our family celebration. We join as a family united in faith, hope, and love.

We are special every day.

Dad asks Michael, "Do you like our new tree house?" Michael answers with a quick "Yes." Dad continues, "A special thanks to Uncle Joe, Marvin, Anthony, Annabelle, Michael, Michelle, and all your cousins for making sure we had the right nails and tools. Flossie, thank you for helping us transport all the lumber. We also cannot forget all the cleanup work done by Mom and Aunt Bess." Michael pipes up, "I found a sleeping bag. Can I sleep in the tree house tonight? Flossie will be here." I say, "So will I. I can give up my bed for one night."

Everyone has a good laugh as they decide on how to take turns sleeping in the family tree house.

Johanna Mckenna

BOOM, BANG, OUCH!

It is the fourth of July! It is hot, and a big parade is coming down Chestnut Street, the town's main street. The high school band kicks things off with the firetrucks, police cars, the Boy Scouts, Girl Scouts, and the veterans in tow. Our neighbor, a veteran of the Spanish-American War, rides in a car. He is too old to walk, but he has a big smile on his face and medals on his chest – as proud as he ever could be!

Annabelle, thirteen years old, is profoundly serious, wearing her black-rimmed glasses, and is carrying the flag for the Girl Scouts. It is heavy, but she is strong and immensely proud to carry the red, white, and blue. Her uncles are veterans of three different wars, WWII and the Korean War. Her grandfather is a veteran of WWI.

They stop at the library on Chestnut Street and Fourth Avenue, where important people will give speeches. The best speech by far was from our pastor, Father O'Brian. He reminded everyone that we would not have a country without God. He told us that we must continue to pray that He keeps our nation safe. We cannot exist without God. Father O'Brian spoke of Rome, Greece, and all the countries that failed without God's help. He reminded us to keep praying and helping each other, especially those in need. He also told us to have an enjoyable time and to enjoy the rest of the day with religious and patriotic fervor.

After the parade, we went back to the farm. We all are staying with Uncle Joe and Aunt Beth at the farm for the summer. As you know, Uncle Joe and Aunt Beth have a huge farm. They have about one hundred cows and sixty chickens. Plus, there is a gigantic vegetable garden—rows upon rows of corn, tomatoes, and other stuff. Aunt Beth has a small herb garden, and she likes to grow parsley, garlic, and carrots… She said they taste good together. I do not know about that. They are real farmers and have five men who work for them.

Flossie is having fun chasing Michael, almost six, in his new red sneakers. I think Turbie, Joe's farm dog, wants to run and play. It looks like he is going to join them in the field. Dad and Uncle Joe hang a big American flag in front of the house. Later today, we are having a Fourth of July celebration. That is when our country became a united country. We became independent and free from English rule. We set up our government and still have a democracy. Dad and Uncle Joe always talk a lot about politics. I hope they talk about something else today.

Flossie just ran into the picnic table. We are in trouble now. Everything is on the ground. "Oh no!" Michael is trying to pick up the watermelon. Flossie and Turbie are eating potato salad. Things are not looking good. Here comes Aunt Beth. She does not look happy. Mom, Dad, and I, Aunt Bess, have arrived. Aunt Beth took charge. "Turbie, go away from here. Go watch the cows, and do not get sick." "Flossie, go with Turbie." "Michael, stand still. The watermelon is still in one piece. Thank Goodness." "As for the potato salad, we will make a different salad and have fresh corn instead. Joe, you, and your brother can set the table back up and let us prepare for our Fourth of July celebration."

Their cousins come running into the field at that exact moment. All uncles and aunts brought their favorite dishes. What a spread. It is a feast, a real celebration. The grill is almost ready when we decide to have a baseball game before we eat. The bases are set up, teams are chosen, and Flossie becomes the umpire. That is a mistake. Flossie has a stomachache, and so does Turbie. They sit and watch the game. Uncle Joe is the pitcher for one team, and Dad will pitch for the other team. I (Aunt Bess) will be the new umpire. "Play ball."

The ninth inning came fast, and there was no score yet. The tension is growing, and so is everyone's hunger—Annabelle swings in. Strike three. "Out!" comes the call. Cousin Paul is up next. Strike one, strike two. Then, a hit. "Run, Paul! Run!" He gets to second base. Michael is next up to bat. "Oh no," the pitcher is thrown; Michael ducks, but too late. The ball gets him right on the shoulder. Now, there is Paul in second. Michael is first, and Gianna, another cousin, is next at bat.

Strike one, strike two, slam! That ball flew! "Run, Paul!" He came in, Michael slid to third, and Gianna got second. "Batter up." Joseph (Gianna's brother) held that bat so tight when he swung with all his might that the ball was out of sight. Gianna runs home, Joseph right behind. Game over! Everybody shook hands, and I declared us all winners in one way or another, even though one team scored more runs. We all played well and had fun. "Yay! That is why Aunt Bess is Aunt Bess, and she is always in charge," exclaims Annabelle. The grill is ready. The celebration is on! Spareribs, chicken, cheeseburgers, hot dogs bigger than a bun, bar-b-que chicken, salad, and so much food. Plus, the chips and dips. Lemonade, soda, and Mom's famous iced tea. And then dessert. Mom has made a flag cake, cupcakes, and lots of ice cream with whipped cream and chocolate syrup—watermelon after the fireworks. Uncle Joe and Dad John are setting up a fireworks display in the open field. There is a split-rail fence that separates the two fields from the house. They both are worried we might be too close.

Fireworks are pretty, but Dad and Uncle Joe think fireworks can also be dangerous. The water hose is nearby. The fireworks are ready to go, and we settle down to watch. Flossie and Turbie are lying right next to the children. The moon is sending sliver beams of light down upon them, our flag blowing gently in the breeze, thoughts of the town parade this morning, baseball game, and banquet. It is the perfect day to celebrate our family, our country and a sense of God's love. We laugh and sing with joy the entire day. The first display goes off with shouts of cheer and excitement. Our neighbors hear the noise and join us on the lawn. Uncle Joe sets off some loud ones that send Flossie and Turbie running to the barn. Their ears are too sensitive to the loud booms and bangs of the fireworks. Robert is trying to sneak into the field where Dad and Uncle Joe lit the display for kids. He almost makes it, but Steve sees him. That cousin of theirs can see in the dark.

We hear a loud "ouch!" from Robert. He will not be trying that again. The grand finale is about to go off. Wow! They lit up the sky and ground. It is magnificent, an actual explosion of color. Mom has the watermelon all sliced up. Everybody enjoys that last bite of celebration as we settle for a night filled with dreams of an American celebration of liberty on the Fourth of July.

Johanna Mckenna

NEVER LET IT GO

I am planting red, white, and yellow tulips by the side of our garage. I have put English Ivy in the window boxes on either side of the door. In front of the windows peeking out of the ground are purple Japanese Iris, thanks to John, my sister's husband. He loves flowers, especially the ones you plant yourselves. It is the joy of seeing something you plant come alive. Flossie, our brown pony, keeps our garage alive. It became her home when I came to live with my sister, Helen, and her family. Annabelle, thirteen years old, wearing her black-rimmed glasses, is excited. She is in charge of the celebration for Michael. He will be six tomorrow. Michelle, eight, is busy blowing up all the balloons. My sister, their mom, is baking a special birthday cake that will look like a baseball. Michael loves to play and watch the games with his dad. I know he will like his cake. My sister is baking extra cupcakes so everyone can have seconds.

Annabelle has invited all her cousins, which is why the party will be at Uncle Joe's farm. Uncle Joe and Aunt Beth enjoy having the family. Plus, they have a big yard where they can play games like baseball, corn hole, and hide and seek. Flossie likes the farm also. Flossie and Turbie chase each other whenever they are there. Michael is going to have his favorite breakfast—pancakes with blueberries and sausages. There will be a big cookout in the afternoon. Michael's favorites are cheeseburgers and grilled hotdogs. Everyone brings something. The children's Aunt Lisa makes the best potato salad. Watermelon is always part of a cookout. Later, the baseball cake will come out with seven candles—six for Michael and one for good luck. Michael will blow them all out. We will share his cake with his favorite chocolate ice cream.

Now come the presents. This is going to be full of surprises for Michael. Uncle Joe and Aunt Beth have a bicycle that is just the right size. Mom and Dad have a new baseball bat and a firetruck he can drive. Annabelle and Michelle have books so he can learn and read about new things. His cousins will have new games, books, and clothes for him. Tomorrow will be fun. I have a firefighter's hat to go with his new firetruck. Flossie seems a little nervous about going this time. I, Aunt Bess, ask, "What is wrong, Flossie? You like going to the farm."

"I need a present for Michael," whispers Flossie.

"Not to worry. Turbie, and you will produce a clever idea." We will leave for the farm right after Michael's special breakfast. We are ready to go by mid-morning. Uncle Joe and Aunt Beth welcomed us with big smiles and open arms. Turbie is waiting for Flossie in the open field. As soon as we park and unload our van, Flossie takes off. The green uncut grass is swaying as the gentle breeze approaches each blade. The warm heat of the sun explodes to welcome us onto the treasured land. Dad always reminds us of the care and love the Native Americans had for this land. "We have to continue to keep this treasure safe. Respect for this gift from God is important. All of God's gifts are important and special." Flossie and Turbie are watching the cows as they head towards the cave. The cave is used as shelter during a storm. They do not need shelter. Instead, they are on a search. Flossie carries a small bucket with her to carry what they hope to find.

They are looking for a special rock to give Michael as their present. Michael has been talking about a shiny rock he saw in the cave last summer. No one thinks it is true except Flossie and Turbie. It has been a while, but they are determined to find the mystery rock. They both think it would be a pleasant birthday surprise for Michael. Turbie runs out to check on the cows while Flossie keeps searching. Flossie is about to give up when she starts digging a little pile of dirt. Turbie runs into the cave, and Flossie jumps. She finds a shiny stone. "This must be it!" Flossie carries it carefully in her bucket to the farmhouse. She gives it to Annabelle, who cannot believe what they have found. She lets out a scream and calls, "Mom, Dad, come look." Aunt Beth and Uncle Joe, wanting to know what was causing all the commotion, join them. Mom Helen starts to cry. "This was my mother's ring. She treasured it and wanted it to remain in the family.

I do not know how it got into the cave. She lost it years ago, but now it is back. Michael will be so excited. I will put it in a little box and wrap it in a birthday present paper for Michael."

Joe yells, "The grill is hot." We join together for a birthday dinner cookout. This is the best cookout we have ever had. Cake and ice cream after some games. Cornhole and baseball are the favorites. "We are so glad we can celebrate together," says Uncle Joe, looking at the children and Aunt Beth. The games end, and out comes the birthday cake with six plus one candles, all lit and ready for Michael. We all sing, "Happy Birthday, Michael," while he blows them out in one big breath. Present time! The bicycle is a big hit, and so is the fire engine. Michael has wonderful gifts. He is blessed to have all this family love. Mom saves the little box for last. Mom tells him how Flossie and Turbie found it. Michael holds the box in his tiny hands. He keeps turning it over and over in his hands. "I do not think I should open it. But I want to see what is inside."

"Michael, I will give you clues. It is old and is a forever gift." Michel slowly unwraps the little box and peers inside. "That is my shiny stone. Someone believed me and found my stone," Michael exclaims. Mom and Dad tell him, "This stone is a diamond from your grandmother's engagement ring. She lost it years ago, and it wound up in the cave. We will never know how that happened, but it is yours now. Michael. This is a precious gift. Grandma wanted her ring to be a part of our family. You found it after all these years. It is yours, but we will save it for you until you are old enough to realize the love and strength of your family."

"We can never let it go."

NEW ADVENTURES

Michael, ten years old, with a mischievous smile on his face and a twinkle in his eyes, is busy collecting eggs. His friend Marcus, also ten, a bit more serious than Michael, is helping him. I, Aunt Bess, am putting eggs in containers by the dozen. Michelle, eleven years old, is supposed to gather enough eggs for our breakfast, but she is busy brushing her hair. She never stops. She thinks it will make it straight. It is not working. Uncle Joe and Aunt Beth have more than two hundred chickens. They sell eggs to people and local stores. Living on Uncle Joe and Aunt Beth's farm has been one adventure after another, but summer is ending. Today is August 16, and their mom and dad are discussing school. Michael pretends not to hear anything about school. School is not on his list of things to do or think about. It is not welcome. During breakfast, Michelle feels a tear sliding down her face. "Michelle, what is wrong?" asks Grandpa Frank.

"I am thinking of school. I do not want to go back. Annabelle will not be there." Annabelle, almost fourteen, graduated from St. Joseph's Elementary School and was awarded a full four-year scholarship to the Christian Academy for Girls. Grandpa Frank explains to Michelle that Annabelle will always be ahead of her in school because she is older. And she will always be her big sister. "Take one day at a time. You will be with Annabelle at her school sooner than you realize."

Pastor Peter and Father David are visiting the farm today. Pastor Peter has gray hair and loves baseball and pizza. Father David is short and has more energy than a lightning bolt. Father David is helping Uncle Joe replace two shingles that had fallen off the roof of the barn during a bad storm. When we look surprised at his abilities, he laughs and says, "You should see the work I did in Vietnam just to survive." They cannot stay long due to their obligations to church. Before they leave, they give us a blessing. Mom and Dad are talking to Aunt Beth and Uncle Joe about the month of September. They both have important meetings and conferences to attend for their work. Annabelle, Michelle, and Michael need new clothes for school and school supplies. Plus, Marcus has to go back home. He misses his mom and dad, and they miss him. Summer was fun, but now it is time for our next adventure.

FLAG DAY

So many years have passed happily. Today is another remarkable day. It is June Fourteenth, Flag Day in the USA. I, Aunt Bess, sit in my double-cushioned rocking chair on the front porch, watching our American flag move with the gentle breeze. I wonder what Michael and Marcus are doing. They look busy doing something in the yard. Lord, help us. One never knows what those two will do next. It will be a surprise. We will be celebrating later with the entire family. Grandpa Frank was in WWI; Uncle Jack was a medic in WWII, and Uncle Gene fought in the Korean War. They called it a conflict, but when men and women die, it is war. I must remind them of all the past generations who helped found our country. It is just a part of me that cannot stop talking. Our past unites us. If children continue to be taught the facts of why our country is so great, our democracy will continue. Michelle, now thirteen, will be entering and joining Annabelle at The Christian Academy for Girls this coming September. Michael will be in seventh grade. They are growing so fast. Annabelle still wants to be a trial lawyer. It is a good thing she likes to study! I know they are receiving a genuine education. Michelle loves to fantasize about her writing. I am so glad her imagination is vivid with scenic portrayals of her choice of characters. Michael is amazing with his knowledge of the Catholic religion. He is an altar server and is serious about his faith. He has the bible memorized. It is just that sometimes, his imagination overtakes "reality." That can be a good thing, sometimes, I think.

It was close to dinner time, and I had promised to help my sister and their mom prepare an American feast. It is not difficult, but it does take time. We baked cornbread this morning. Three loaves should be delicious. Dad is in charge of the smoked turkey, while Michelle is shucking the corn. Annabelle is responsible for dessert, which has to be apple pie. Of course, there will be an American flag cake. That leaves the children's mother, and me with a variety of dishes to choose from. We decide on macaroni and cheese, broccoli, carrot salad, and watermelon. Michael insists on the American hotdog and hamburgers with French fries. It is a good thing the cousins are coming. Father David and Pastor Peter are invited. I know they will pray an amazing grace before dinner. Michael runs into the house, "Come quickly, there is a fire." We run outside to see a massive fire with smoke drifting into what is a blue sky.

"Michal, why did you frighten us? This is a large fire in the fire pit. It is under control (I hope)."

"Look over by the garage. We have set up an army camp. Grandpa Frank told us how to do it. He told us about his time during WWI. He was a scout in the forests of Germany. They used to sleep on the ground, in makeshift shelters, or in the open. They only slept in the afternoon and had to take turns sleeping only one to two hours at night. They used to light fires when they could, but most of the time, they were cold and hungry. This fire is extra big because Grandpa Frank wanted to get warm. Thinking about the war made him remember the cold nights spent in fear of capture or death. It was seldom possible to have a good fire. So, he wants it now. He wants to be warm."

"Dad, why are they afraid to teach our history in public school? My friends were telling me they do not know anything about our country."

Annabelle is telling us about the world wars, the conflicts, and what is happening in our country now. Her Social Studies teacher was in the Marines and is extremely proud of our country. Mr. Johnson tells us there is no other country in the world that allows the freedoms that we have. He also says that we must study and learn about our past accomplishments. Everyone can succeed in our country if they have faith, work hard, and persevere. We have to take advantage of the opportunities offered to us. He also tells us that when we decide on our career choice, "Be happy at what you are going to do for the rest of your life; you must like what you are going to do. That does not mean you have to become a millionaire. Money does not guarantee happiness. Money is important because you have to be able to support yourself and, God willing, eventually your family."

Michelle adds to the conversation. She tells us that her friends all ask the same questions. "Why is everyone worried about their color? And what sex are they? I was born a girl and white. Marcus is black and a boy. He is Michael's best friend, and we are good friends with his parents. You are a man, and your mom is a woman. We are a family just like Marcus has his family." Mr. Johnson tells us directly, "I am a man, and I am an American of African ancestry, which is why I am Black. We are not a racist country. There are people in our country who are racists, but as a country, we are a blend of nationalities who get along quite well."

Michael says, "All we did was set up an army camp, and now you are all so serious. What happened?" Dad answers, "You reminded us of the sacrifices our young men and women made to help keep our country free." Dad also reminds us that Grandpa Frank was an immigrant from Sicily. He was fifteen years old when he came to our country's promise of a future. He did not speak English. At that time, you had to have a sponsor and promise of employment. His brother, Mike, sponsored him, and he was hired as a cutter in the Norwich knitting mills in Norwich, New York. Grandpa Frank went to night school to learn English, and eventually, he opened his own business and bank accounts and bought his own house. He proudly displayed the American flag.

Everyone stops talking as suddenly we hear loud noises coming from Marcus's yard. We all ran over to see if everything was all right. We find Marcus and his father lying on the grass. They are laughing so hard and loud it sounds as if a herd of elephants has come pounding through. Marcus tells us they were trying to hang a giant banner when it fell, and they got wrapped up in it. It was Flag Day, and when Marcus stood, he was wrapped in the stars. His dad is going to put him next to the stripes. It is decided to hang the banner in both our front yards, which run together. We are celebrating Flag Day together as all

Americans should. We decided to sleep outside that night in the camp Michael and Marcus had put together. Grandpa Frank says, "That is how it was." Dad and Mom both agree that the new so-called Left political shift of our country should try it for a night. "They are so spoiled I do not think they can survive the entire night."

The cousins, uncles, and aunts descend at that moment. Now the celebration begins. Baseball is first. Teams are chosen, and let the game begin! Dad has the smoked turkey ready to carve, hot dogs, and everything else is ready as soon as the game ends. Pastor Peter and Father David both arrive a little out of breath. We ask, "What is wrong? You both seem distraught." "We are. The church was vandalized last night. The tabernacle was broken into, and two of our statues were spray-painted and smashed. The police are investigating. This is considered a hate crime." This is hard to believe. We do not live in the city. This is considered a country and a typical middle-class town. This is still America. How could this happen? These kinds of things just do not happen here. Grandpa Frank says, "These things, as you call them, happen everywhere and anywhere the devil reigns. If there is sin, evil that predominates the country, evil will prevail in people's thoughts and deeds. Remember Germany. They had an evil leader who destroyed their country and other countries. People were persecuted and killed because they did not agree with him. Look at our country. If you disagree with the so-called left, you are persecuted. They come after you if you believe in life. We can send our children to a Catholic or a private religious school, or we can teach them at home, which is a blessing. The young children in government schools are not taught about our history and the good that America has brought to the world. The lives of young Americans that were lost and damaged to help others. These young people know nothing of the struggles necessary to maintain our way of life. The students should study all the ancient civilizations that destroyed themselves. We are the worst civilization that has ever existed, and soon, our civilization will be part of history. God help us."

"I will not be alive when the ravages of war happen in this country. I pray with confidence, but it is difficult to eliminate the knowledge of turmoil existing within humans. It prevails within me, not for myself but for the innocent children born out of love. Treasure the moments of life, the joys of innocent childhood, and the blessings God has given us. Fight for the truth; God always triumphs. Stay with the truth. Be not afraid."

"That was quite a speech," says Dad. "Both of you, Aunt Bess and Grandpa Frank, I believe all you told us, but how do we make the American people wake up? They are content to go along with the crowd, right or wrong." Pastor Peter and Father David both say, "Pray with all your soul, heart, and mind. We think we should celebrate Flag Day right now." We agree—enough talking for now.

The game ends, Dad completes slicing the smoked turkey, and all the food is ready. We sit at the table where we join hands for a family blessing from Pastor Peter. Father David leads us in grace before our meal, which is patriotic and devout.

Johanna Mckenna

SCHOOL BEGINS

Annabelle, wearing her dark-rimmed glasses and dressed in her new uniform, green suit, white blouse, brown shoes with white socks, is waiting for the forty-nine bus. She is standing on the corner of Chestnut Street and Second Avenue. It is about an hour's ride to her new school. As the bus approaches, she has this feeling of the unknown. Annabelle steps onto the bus, not frightened by her new life but with a sense of trepidation. The unknown is to be investigated and dealt with in a positive manner. The bus stops, and she jumps out and looks at a group of young girls standing in front of a small building. Annabelle hopes to become a lawyer in the future. This school might be small, but actual academics prevail. Annabelle is a serious student and is looking forward to new knowledge. She hopes to become a trial lawyer.

Michelle, entering sixth grade, will study American history. She will be learning about the courage of our ancestors who fought in every war, not only for our own country but for other countries who needed help to fight evil. This year, I, her Aunt Bess, can help her. I was a history major at Catholic University in D.C. Michael and his friend Marcus are both in fifth grade. They line up, take their assigned seats, and are given new books. The first one they open is mathematics. "Oh No," thinks Michael. "This is not a good beginning. It is a whole page of word problems."

Michael likes to read the problems but does not like to do the work involved in solving the problem. Marcus looks at them and laughs. He loves numbers. They jumble around in his head, and somehow, he begins to understand how they work together. It is a good thing they can help each other. Michael becomes more interested in the weather than in schoolwork. He wants it to snow. Michael wants to build an airplane. He is wondering how to make an airplane out of snow. How can he make the wings stay in the air? Suddenly, he hears his name, "Michael, pay attention. Come back to Earth." It is Mrs. Mirk's strict voice. Michael thinks, "How does Mrs. Mirk know I am not paying attention? She must have eyes in the back of her head. I better listen; I will never understand this work." Michael's thoughts then turn to Grandpa Frank. He thinks Grandpa Frank is right. He always tells me, "You have to learn mathematics if you want to fly an airplane. Angels have wings, and you do not!"

Finally, the weekend arrives. Saturday morning, Michael's dad decides we should all run for health reasons. Exercise is good for us. He is right, but I, Aunt Bess, am twenty-nine! I will do something else besides running. "Too old," I think to myself. Saturday afternoon, I found Annabelle doing research with books and her computer. Her long-term homework assignment is to study and compare the ancient civilizations of Greece, Rome, Egypt, and others to our so-called civilization. Have we learned from the past? Are we repeating the same mistakes? Have we improved? Or become worse? How are we the same, and how should or could we improve? Michael and Marcus are working on math problems. Michael reads the problem, and Marcus explains the numbers. They are doing well until Michael decides to make a paper airplane. He is folding his paper, trying to make an airplane. Grandpa Frank says, "Michael, let me show you the right way. Fold the paper in half-length wise. Then, fold the top corners. Fold the paper on both sides so they are even. Fold them right to the center of the paper." Mom Is looking at them, "This is a waste of time and too confusing." Annabelle looks up and says, "Let me try. This looks interesting." She folds the paper the right way, and it flies across the room. She bows, and she receives a burst of applause.

"Well done," exclaims Grandpa Frank. "Michael, someday you might fly your own airplane. Did you know the first airplane was built by two brothers? Orville and Wilbur Wright. They heard of the glider plane built by a German engineer, Otto Lilienthal, in 1890. They experimented with gliders and failed, but they kept on trying. Their first plane flew on December 17th, 1903, in Kitty Hawk, South Carolina." Grandpa Frank is telling us about the time he visited Kitty Hawk, standing on the hill where the first plane took off. They have a small museum. Grandpa Frank remembers standing by the fence receiving the devastating news that our country, America, had been attacked. "Nine Eleven." September 11th, 2001. Receiving this news was more overwhelming than being where the first airplane took off. Grandpa Frank is telling us this with tears running down his face. I never saw him look like this. All he could say was, "War is the result of sin. Evil begets evil."

He shakes his head and, with a smile, comes back from sad memories. He reminds Annabelle, Michelle, Michael, and Marcus that the future of our country is in their hands. Study and learn. "Back to your studies, everyone. Finish your homework." Michelle is engrossed in her current reading. For extra credit, she is reading about our Constitution and John Adams. He was our second president and knew about government. He said, "Democracy has to be taken care of by honest men. If the people in charge are not honest, we would not be a democracy anymore." "Grandpa Frank, is he right?" asks Michelle. "Yes. He is. We will talk about that later. This is the reason you must study and learn about your country. The United States is still a young country, but we have accomplished more in our time than has ever been done. We must live by God's rules; otherwise, we will fall apart. There is no negotiating on this topic. There is right vs wrong, good vs evil. Only The Truth will keep us free."

Suddenly, Willie, Marcus's shaggy dog, can be heard barking. We run to see what is happening. Flossie, our family pet, the pony, is right by his side. Flossie has been sick for four days with a bad cold. The veterinarian gave her medicine, and Michelle has been taking care of her. Michelle wants to be a nurse. She is reading about Sue Barton, an extraordinary nurse who helps her patients get better quickly. Michelle knows Sue Barton is not a real person, but Michelle has a cousin, Kim, who is a real nurse. She wants to be like her. Annabelle is the first to say, "Good job, Michelle. Flossie looks all better." Mom and Dad are outside making sure the house and yard are ready for the coming winter weather. They asked us if we wanted to join them for a game of touch football. Grandpa Frank answers, "Why not? We need fresh air." That is decided; Annabelle, Michelle, and Michael run outside for a welcome break from homework. Grandpa Frank and I walk out to watch.

A brisk sunny day, perfect weather to be outside. I am thinking when Flossie takes off with the football in her mouth. Trotting down the street with Willie alongside her and Michael, Michelle, Annabelle, Mom, and Dad right behind her makes quite a sight, a ridiculous one. Marcus, his mom, and his dad come outside when they hear the noise. They join them in the chase for Flossie and the football. Grandpa Frank and I cannot stop laughing. Flossie takes them around the block and trots right back to our house. She drops the football and proceeds to go back to her pony house, our two-car heated garage. Willie follows her. Everyone starts to laugh, and Dad says, "That is enough exercise for today. Tomorrow is Sunday, and we will attend early Mass so that you can complete your work after church."

Johanna Mckenna

FALL HOLIDAYS

Ten o'clock Mass is the goal of the morning. Michael is the altar server for this Mass, and Pastor Peter is the celebrant. We bless ourselves, enter the church of St. Joseph the Carpenter, and take our seats near the front of the church. Pastor Peter is giving his homily, which catches the attention of all his parishioners. He is more serious than usual. The topic is about the holidays that will be coming. Listing them all, he begins with Halloween, explaining the true meaning of Hollow's Eve. "Think of dressing your children as saints or angels. Stay away from the devil and witches. Cowboys, Cowgirls, Police, Firefighters, anything that is good, not evil. We are fighting evil in our world. It is the day before All Saints Day, and your children can have fun dressing up in costume portraying their favorite saint." Pastor Peter is also telling us about Thanksgiving. "Try to do something for the homeless and those in need. Go the extra mile. Do something special for others in need of food and clothes." He says he will talk about Christmas later in the year. He ends with the thought, "Remember, put yourselves in the person's shoes."

As soon as we arrive back home, Annabelle begins working on her research project. Michelle is almost finished with her report on John Adams, and Michael is nowhere to be seen. Mom is in the kitchen preparing dinner when the phone rings. It is their Uncle Joe. They all stop working and start listening, secretly hoping he invites them for Thanksgiving. Uncle Joe says, "I know this is early to be thinking of Thanksgiving, but we want to be sure you will be here for the American holiday. This year is important. We still have a country if God is our focal point. We must celebrate our freedom and way of life." He takes Mom by surprise. She is thinking, "First Pastor Peter, and now Uncle Joe. Why is everyone rushing the holidays this year?" Dad shakes his head, "Yes." So, Mom says, "OK. But we have to bring something to help with dinner. Aunt Beth gets on the phone and asks for Marcus' phone number. They want to invite Marcus and his parents. "That sounds exciting," thinks Mom. "Wait until Michael hears this," says Dad. "This is going to be a busy Fall."

He was right. September came and went quickly. Grandpa Frank tells Michael he can be St. Michael and carry a sword for All Hallow's Eve. I, Aunt Bess, call my sister's husband, John, because this way, everyone knows who I am talking about. I call my sister Helen because I like how it sounds. I even refer to Beth as Aunt Beth and Joe as Uncle Joe because my stories are all about and for these beautiful children, and I love them more when they so intently listen to me telling them. So, Mom is thinking about how she can make costumes for Michael and Michelle. Michelle wants to be St. Lucy, the patron saint of eyes. "Protect my eyes so I may see the beauty of creation, the shining sun, and the smile of a child," Mom says that prayer all the time. She taught that to Annabelle because she has to wear glasses. Schoolwork keeps Annabelle, Michelle, and Michael busy; they do not realize it is Hollow's Eve. Their costumes are ready. Marcus is going to be Gabriel, another Archangel to help Michael. The school decides to have the parents form a big circle in the parking lot with their cars and have a "trunk or treat" party. Grandpa Frank is telling us how when he was a child, even their mom and dad used to go from house to house, ringing doorbells for "trick or treat." It was fun, but this is fun also. Grandpa Frank always says, "Time goes fast when you are having fun."

November is here already! Marcus is as excited as we are. Going to Uncle Joe's farm is special for him. I, Aunt Bess, enjoy being at the farm. Children think Aunt Beth is a little bossy, but she does everything in such a way that we laugh a lot. The week moves quickly, and on Thursday, Thanksgiving is here before we can turn around. "Aunt Bess, do not forget the cookies," Annabelle had told me. I will not forget the cookies. I hope the guests at the dinner enjoy them. Mom and Dad are hurrying everyone into their van. We are helping cook and serve Thanksgiving dinner to guests from the shelter. Annabelle is glad we made cookies. I wish we had made more cookies. Dinner is over, cleanup is finished, and soon we are on our way back home. Our van and Marcus's Mom and Dad's vans are both filled with great anticipation for our family. Thanksgiving celebration is great.

Flossie and Willie are with us. They have a special trailer hooked onto our van where they can stand and lie down. The farm is in Pennsylvania and about three hours from our home. Michelle thinks it would be fun if we pretended to be pilgrims traveling to a new destination. She makes it sound exciting and dangerous, which is for the real pilgrims. They traveled for sixty-five days and were sick for most of the trip. At least her talking made the trip go faster. Uncle Joe and Aunt Beth await us with open arms and big smiles. The dancing flames of the big fireplace greet us as we walk into the farmhouse.

The van is unloaded, and the darkness of night soon envelops us as we relax for our first evening at the farm. Flossie and Willie have a special stall in the barn just for them. Sitting by the fireplace, enjoying Aunt Beth's sandwiches, we talk about tomorrow when the rest of our family arrives. They are all farmers and live near Uncle Joe and Aunt Beth. Grandpa Frank speaks loudly and clearly, "I am tired and want to go to bed." We are all tired. It has been a long day, and tomorrow will be busy. We all agree that we need a good night's sleep. We wake up to a loud noise. Our relatives have arrived and are ready to celebrate this American holiday.

Michael and Marcus are with their cousins, uncles, and aunts. Aunt Beth and "Mom" have a big country breakfast ready. Blueberry pancakes with pure maple syrup, bacon, eggs, toast, coffee, tea, milk, fresh fruit, juice, and joy. Grandpa Frank starts to tear up but then smiles and soon has a plateful of pancakes with syrup on his plate. Grandpa Frank leads us in the blessing before meals and tells us, "This is our first celebration without Grandma. I see tears in your eyes. I am sad also, but we must remember all the joy and recipes your grandma left us. Grandma wants you to have a good Christian life. I know her secret ingredient. It was and still is "Love." She loved cooking for her family; she did it with love. You and I will see her again if we follow the Ten Commandments of God. They are our gateway to heaven." After that heartfelt message, through our tears, we smile and sit to enjoy our breakfast with our own special memories of Grandma. She will always be with us. Uncle Joe has built a special table for our family. It is long and takes up two rooms. It sits our whole family. Remember, Dad has eight brothers, and Michael has twenty-two cousins. After breakfast, the men, including Michael and Marcus, go outside to help him cut down a tree, spread mulch, and do whatever work has to be done. Michael and Marcus decide they are going to find a giant pumpkin so Aunt Beth can make a pumpkin pie. They quietly disappear to go on a search for the best and biggest pumpkin. The women help in the kitchen and begin preparing dinner.

As they are working, Aunt Beth wants to hear about school life and what they are learning. She is especially curious about Annabelle, her first year in the academy. Annabelle tells her about Latin and French. Her teacher was born in France and lived there until she was sixteen. She can only speak French in her classroom, and the class might go on a class trip to France in the Spring of next year. Michelle wants to become a nurse to help people get better when they become sick. All her book reports are about Sue Barton.

"This is one of the special moments of my life, sitting with my loved ones, laughing, talking, and dreaming about the past, present, and future of our family and our country," I'm thinking to myself.

Pastor Peter and Father David are invited for dinner. Father David is excited. He has never celebrated Thanksgiving before. He exclaims, "I am really beginning to feel American, my first turkey dinner." Grandpa Frank asked them if they would say Mass for the family before dinner, so they came well prepared. As the family gathers for a special Mass of Thanksgiving, Michael and Marcus show up in a wagon with a giant pumpkin. They tell Aunt Beth, "It is too heavy to carry, but we thought it would make a great pie." She laughs and tells them, "That pumpkin will make more than one pie. We will have muffins, cookies, and more. Do you realize we have to cook the pumpkin first?" Michael looks sad, but Aunt Beth says, "Do not worry. We will get it done. There are workers in my kitchen." Pastor Peter tells Michael, "You are just in time. Help us fix the altar and Aunt Beth's dining room table, and then we can begin. Pastor Peter and Father David celebrate Mass together, bringing enough Blessed Hosts for everyone to receive communion.

I think, "This is truly the beginning of a Thanksgiving celebration. God and Family, what a team! We, as a family, are blessed."

The kitchen becomes the focus of attention. The delicious aromas of the turkeys, the stuffing, plus all the trimmings make us realize the depth of our hunger. Mom, joined by the other women, gets busy setting the table. This is quite a chore because we are a large group. Uncle Joe set up another table for all the cousins to sit together with, you guessed it, Grandpa Frank. Pastor Peter says the blessing before meals, "Bless us, Oh Lord, for these YOUR gifts, which we are about to receive through YOUR bounty."

Everyone is warm, happy, laughing, and sharing stories of things done and undone. It becomes serious at one point when Aunt Joan announces she is retiring at the end of this school year. She cannot, in good conscience, teach the lies being taught in the public/government schools. "I have one little boy who decides to be a girl on Monday, so I am to call him by the pronoun she or her. The children are confused, but it is wrong to expose them to such craziness because of political agenda." Aunt Joan continues, "I cannot be a part of the evil that is being perpetrated in our society." We agree with her but decided to keep the conversation away from politics, at least for now. Michelle tells her, "You can teach at our school. That will be fun." Aunt Joan says, "That is a promising idea, and I will investigate it." Pastor Peter is telling Aunt Joan they need strong teachers in our school. "It is becoming an immoral, evil world. The children must be prepared. They must be taught the truth and given the knowledge to ward off today's culture." Grandpa Frank has the cousins' table laughing at his stories. Father David says the blessing after we finish dinner,

"Thanking God for the gifts we have received." The cousins are ready for a football game after dinner. We all need a break. The dishes are piled high, and it will take a long time to clean up the kitchen. Dad, his brothers, Pastor Peter, and Father David quietly head towards the TV to watch a football game. The men are relaxed until Willie comes running in and jumps on Father David's lap. Willie is a big, shaggy dog, too big for a lap dog. The jump takes us all by surprise, especially Father David. He jumps and then laughs at Willie. Willie is put back outside to play football with the cousins. Flossie is watching everything and everyone. She sees Willie, and they unite to join the football game. Flossie and Willie cause chaos on the front lawn chasing the football. It is when they run away with the football. "Game over" is called. The game on TV ends. At the same moment, a voice is heard, "Dessert Time," calls Aunt Beth. That works out! Aunt Beth is right, and she has the pumpkin cooked and turned into three delicious pies with whipped cream on top. Apple pies, cakes, cookies, and every type of pastry are more than delicious. Each family brings a dish plus a dessert. Pastor Peter and Father David tell the family they would like to say the Rosary with the family before it is time to leave.

During dinner, Pastor Peter and Father David discuss the March for Life in January. They ask us to help prepare and pray for March's success. We pray for the rosary, asking Our Lady to intercede for us. They tell us there will be a meeting to organize the trip to Washington D.C. After the Rosary, our uncles, aunts, cousins, Pastor Peter, and Father David depart for their homes. We stay for the weekend, which moves swiftly, and soon, we are on our way back to our home in New Jersey.

LESSONS LEARNED

There is a new boy in Michael's class who does not look friendly. Michael remembers Pastor Peter and Grandpa Frank telling him to put himself in that person's shoes and see how he would feel. Michael thinks about it. "I would be scared coming into a new building and meeting new people. I bet he feels the same way." Michael's teacher, Mrs. Mirk, has a buddy system in her classroom. She wants her students to learn to help others. Mrs. Mirk introduces Greg to her class. She asks Michael and Marcus to be Greg's friends. Greg sits next to Michael in his new classroom. He sits next to Michael and Marcus for lunch. The three of them start laughing because the peanut butter sandwiches stick to the roofs of their mouths. Greg, with short black, curly hair, likes baseball and airplanes. His dad is an airplane pilot in the Air Force. The three soon become "The Three Musketeers." They are planning things to do, but first, they have to study for a history test on the Constitution of the United States of America. Mrs. Mirk tells them, "They must learn history because if it is good, we can do the same thing. If it is not good, we should not repeat the same mistake." We can hear her sometimes when she is thinking aloud, "Why is history being repeated? Ours will not be the first civilization to fail. People never learn."

On his way home, Michael tells Marcus he wants to go on the March for Life. Marcus tells Michael, "You better find out what it is about and ask your mom and dad if you can go all the way to Washington, D.C. Michael walks in the door and is greeted by Mom, who is on her way to a meeting. They have to raise money to pay for the bus in January. She has an idea that she wants to share with the group of volunteers. Pastor Peter listens to all the ideas for fundraising. He likes the idea of a Parish Italian dinner—homemade tomato sauce, meatballs, pasta, garlic bread, salad, and dessert. The adults will make the dinners, and the young members of the parish will set up and serve. A nominal fee will be charged, and they can have it on two different nights. It sounds exciting and work. When

Michael hears about the plan, he tells Marcus and Greg. They are the first to volunteer. Mom organized it already. Mom has the flyers printed, and they will be in the bulletin next week. We need all parishioners to help with this project. There are four Saturdays, and we will use the last two Saturdays before Christmas. Michael, Marcus, and Greg team up and deliver flyers to every student in school, plus they are in the bulletin. The phone is off the hook; people want to help.

It is time for tomato sauce. Mom has a recipe printed and available for anyone who needs it. The Knights of Columbus of the parish will make meatballs at the school cafeteria the night before the dinners. The cooks will bring their tomato sauce into the cafeteria by ten o'clock Saturday morning. Pour the sauce into giant pots, add the meatballs, and put on simmer for four hours. The Junior Knights are responsible for the set-up of all the tables and clean up after dinner. Grandpa Frank is going to be the speaker, along with Pastor Peter. During all this activity, Annabelle, Michelle, and Michael must keep up with their studies, which they are doing. Annabelle is in the midst of learning how to argue her position on a topic with intelligent discourse; she is learning how to debate. Her topic is Pro-life against Pro-choice. She is becoming well-versed on the topic. She is presenting the pro-life side of the debate against a pro-abortion challenger. Michelle is developing her writing skills; the choice of topics is interesting. She has to author an essay on one of the following: 1.The Best Experience of Your Life. 2.Lessons You learned from your Grandparents. 3.Your first experience swimming or hiking. 4.Something important you learned or did at church. 5.Write about Your experience with Race. 6.Your Favorite Vacation. 7.Write about the similarities and differences between another country and American life. 8.Write about Love. 9.Write about forgiveness. 10.Write about your feet: where have they been? And where are they going?

Mr. Smith, Michelle's teacher, allows and encourages the class to have parents, grandparents, and others help them research their chosen topic. The students have to give facts and truth in their writing. They must acknowledge with quotation marks who, what, where, and how they received their information. Michelle thinks, "This is more complicated than I thought it would be." Michael is about to embark on a new adventure. Mrs. Mirk gives the students a list of ideas. They must choose one to work on and complete it in time for the science fair. Two students can work on one project. Michael looks at Marcus and Greg. Michael asks Mrs. Mirk if they can work together. Mrs. Mirk says, "Yes, you can work together since Greg is still new to the class." A list of ideas is on the board, and Michael wants to do the one 'building an airplane from clothespins and popsicle sticks.' The challenge is to make it fly. Marcus and Greg think it is an excellent choice. The challenge is on! Michael, Marcus, and Greg are busy completing their project. It must be painted and able to fly. They are determined and will succeed. Grandpa Frank is practicing his presentation for dinner. November 4 is the first dinner, and they are sold out. This Friday is meatball night. Plus, there are sixty-two orders to be picked up. The Knights, volunteer workers, and Pastor Peter made the dinner an enormous success. All our family will be helping at the dinner. We all want to hear Grandpa Frank. He has been practicing on our pets, Flossie and Willie. They did not make too much noise; it was either they liked what he said, or they just liked Grandpa Frank. He does give them lovely treats at least twice a day.

Saturday, November fourth. Show-time. Tables are set, food is hot and ready to go. Michael, dressed as St. Michael, the Archangel, is greeting the people as they arrive. Marcus, also dressed as an Archangel, is handing out programs when the people are seated. Greg is playing the piano, and Michelle is going to sing later. Annabelle is in charge of the cousins, who are helping as servers. It is time for Grandpa to speak about the reason this dinner is so important. When he led us in the blessing before we had dinner, Pastor Peter spoke a little about the March to Life. He told us Grandpa Frank would tell us more later when he gave his presentation. Grandpa Frank stands before a captivated audience and begins, "I am joining the Pro-life group this year in Washington, D.C. I knew about the March, but never helped enough. This year, we must join the March for Life. Someone in my family told me that I was too old. I told him that the road to Calvary was long also. I am going along with all my family. We are committed to saving babies. We have not learned from the past civilizations of Greece, Rome, Egypt, and others. When we stop learning from the past, we become barbarians and kill our people. We as a nation are committing the greatest crime against humanity and doing it for ourselves. The killing of babies pre-born and born is evil, the work of Lucifer. It is taught the final destruction of humankind would be the destruction of the family by the devil. It is happening. We have evil leaders, but we can never give up. God will win, but we must show our love for Him by doing what is right. This year, our church is sponsoring two buses to join the March for Life: thanks to all of you. We have been created with a body and soul made in the image and likeness of God. We must show the world we are dedicated and united to save innocent lives from torture and ultimate death. It is killing, against the fifth commandment of our God." Father David joins Grandpa Frank with a final word. "We must protect life. It is a gift from God. How do you feel when you give someone you love a gift and are rejected? Not too good; think of the tears shed by Jesus and His mother every time a new baby is killed. Join us; this is the greatest crime ever committed in our century. You are needed. We must show our strength and love by uniting with all who believe in the truth."

The dinners raise enough money for three buses that are filled. Annabelle's school joins us on the trip while Michael, Marcus, and Greg lead the Rosary at their school. The awareness brought on by the March for Life made everyone acknowledge the severe problems facing our nation and the world. Annabelle, Michelle, Michael, Marcus, and Greg are proud of their work. They should be. They are young leaders of today and tomorrow. This was a lesson, "Learning that fighting for the truth is not easy." Annabelle, Michelle, and Michael are back in school, facing the winter storms of weather and school. Michelle is happy that the principal is evaluating her writing.

Sister Elizabeth wants to enter her newest essay in the state competition. She wrote, "Face-to-face communications is beyond repair due to social networking." Michelle writes her opinion. She does not think it is beyond repair. Her faith does not let her think negatively. She is convinced people do communicate with each other. I, Aunt Bess, know this family does.

Annabelle is engrossed in learning Latin. She tells Grandpa Frank that she heard Latin was a dead language. Grandpa Frank tells her, "Never, Latin is the universal language of our church. People come and go, but the church will always be here." Michael says, "We had only one snowstorm this winter. I want it to snow today." Grandpa Frank reminds him, "We cannot always get what we want, and there is always a good reason for that. We may not like it, but that is too bad because that is how it should be. Life was not meant to be easy or to get what we wanted. Finish your work. That is more important than snow." Michael lets out a groan but continues working on his latest assignment in Geography. He is learning how to read maps of different countries. Grandpa Frank asks him, "Where are Italy and Greece, and where are we? Where is Ireland, and what waters are near each country?" Michael becomes interested. He wants to know where his ancestors came from.

The months become busy with continued schoolwork and small snowstorms. Winter is closing the door as Spring knocks on our windows. The daffodils are bursting forth, ignoring the cold. It is their time to bring the blessing of Spring. The forsythias are in bloom, and baseball. Spring training begins—Mets, Yankees, and Grandpa's favorite, the Dodgers. Grandpa Frank grew up in Brooklyn and played in the minor league for the Brooklyn Dodgers. He still has good memories of his team. Grandpa Frank's pitching arm is bent in a funny position because he broke it playing a game. The doctors set it incorrectly, and he could no longer play for the team. Grandpa Frank does love the game of baseball. Michael likes playing catch with him. He is learning the correct way to hold the bat, run, and slide into the bases; all there is to know about baseball. Michelle is taking care of our pet, who finally wants to be outside. Flossie, our pet pony, is getting older by the day and does not like wintry weather. She is comfortable in her house, our two-car heated garage. The weather is warmer now, and she wants to join Michael and Grandpa. Annabelle is busy with her schoolwork and preparing to become the editor of the school paper the next school year. She has won two writing awards this year, which is quite an accomplishment. I, Aunt Bess, am sitting by a large window overlooking the backyard. I see Grandpa Frank showing Michael the correct way to bat and the best way to throw a pitch. Michelle is brushing our pet pony, Annabelle is reading her latest book, "Destiny of the Republic" by 'Candice Millard.' Annabelle does like history. I see Marcus running to join them. Mom, my sister, and Dad, my brother-in-law, are enjoying the day. They must be planning their garden for the Summer. This has been a busy and learning year. Next year, Annabelle will be in her second year at the Academy, Michelle will be in seventh grade, and Michael will be in sixth grade. They are growing so fast. Marcus went home to get Willie; he was also growing older by the minute. The shaggy dog is a little gray when you look closely. I am getting younger, but Grandpa Frank is getting older.

I better stop daydreaming and join my family. It is a time to be happy and thank God for all we have. We must pray that God willing, their future will be safe, and they can make their mark upon the world. New adventures are ahead for Annabelle, Michelle, Michael, their mom and dad, and me, Aunt Bess.